W9-CBS-346

Also by Julia Child

Mastering the Art of French Cooking, Volume I
(with Simone Beck and Louisette Bertholle)

The French Chef Cookbook

Mastering the Art of French Cooking, Volume II
(with Simone Beck)

From Julia Child's Kitchen

The Way to Cook

Cooking with Master Chefs

In Julia's Kitchen with Master Chefs

Julia's Breakfasts, Lunches, and Suppers

Julia's Breakfasts, Lunches, and Suppers

by Julia Child

In collaboration with E. S. Yntema

Photographs by James Scherer

Alfred A. Knopf   New York   1999

This Is a Borzoi Book
Published by Alfred A. Knopf, Inc.

Copyright © 1999 by Julia Child
All rights reserved under International and Pan-
American Copyright Conventions. Published in the
United States by Alfred A. Knopf, Inc., New York, and
simultaneously in Canada by Random House of
Canada Limited, Toronto. Distributed by Random
House, Inc., New York.
www.randomhouse.com

The recipes in this book were originally published in the
books *Julia Child & Company* and *Julia Child & More
Company,* which were published by Alfred A. Knopf,
Inc., in 1978 and 1979 respectively. Copyright © 1978
(*Julia Child & Company*) and copyright © 1979 (*Julia
Child & More Company*) by Julia Child. These two
books were also released in a single edition as *Julia
Child's Menu Cookbook,* published in 1991 by Wings
Books, distributed by Outlet Book Company, Inc., a
Random House Company, by arrangement with Alfred
A. Knopf, Inc.

"Soup for Supper" appeared in somewhat shorter form
in *McCall's.*

Knopf, Borzoi Books, and the colophon are registered
trademarks of Random House, Inc.

Library of Congress Cataloging-in-Publication Data
Child, Julia.
    Julia's breakfasts, lunches, and suppers / by Julia
Child, in collaboration with E. S. Yntema ; photographs
by James Scherer. — 1st ed.
        p.   cm.
    Includes index.
    ISBN 0-375-40339-6 (hc.)
    1. Cookery.   2. Menus.   I. Yntema, E. S.   II. Title.
TX715.C545625   1999
642'.4—dc21   98-38186
                                                          CIP

Manufactured in the United States of America
First Edition

Contents

Acknowledgments

This is a book of menus drawn from our television series *Julia Child & Company* and its sequel, *Julia Child & More Company*. The recipes for the complete series appeared in two separate books, were then all collected into one big book, and are now split into four convenient smaller books, of which this is the fourth volume.

The series was produced for public television at WGBH TV in Boston, with Russell Morash as producer/director in association with Ruth Lockwood. The food designer and recipe developer was Rosemary Manell, who worked closely with our photographer, James Scherer. Marian Morash, chef for the popular *This Old House,* was also executive chef for us. I count us fortunate indeed to have had E. S. Yntema as a writer. Peggy Yntema's wit and spirit always make for good reading.

It takes a peck of people to put on shows such as these, and other members of our team at one time or another included Gladys Christopherson, Bess Coughlin, Wendy Davidson, Bonnie Eleph, Jo Ford, Temi Hyde, Sara Moulton, Pat Pratt, John Reardon, Bev Seamons, and, of course, our able makeup artist, Louise Miller. I have not mentioned the technicians, camera crew, and lighting engineers, or our book designer, Chris Pullman, or our favorite editor at Knopf, Judith Jones.

Introduction

This is the fourth in our series of menu books. The other three contain menus, ideas, and recipes for informal dinners, special occasions, and family meals. We are more informal with our meals in this book, and include a good number of old favorites. To start off our Breakfast Party, as an example, we offer eggs Benedict, including instructions for poaching an egg and mastering a hollandaise sauce. For this same party you'll find out how to make your own corned beef hash and your own English muffins. A real French onion soup highlights Soup for Supper, and a splendid lobster soufflé served on a platter makes its appearance for an important luncheon party. Other notables include a real New England potluck supper with its hearty fish chowder, its traditional cole slaw, and that famous pilgrim dessert, Indian pudding. If you are looking for a really superior American potato salad, you'll find it in the Holiday Lunch, where you'll also find an amusing pâté known as Chicken Melon. The Sunday Night Supper is a great boiled dinner with plenty of steamed vegetables and a garlic-horseradish sauce all served over your own homemade noodles.

As with all the menus in this series, you are given the full story — not only detailed recipes for each dish, but shopping lists, timing suggestions, alternative choices, wines to serve — in fact you will find everything you need to produce an entertaining and delicious meal. Because the book is fully indexed, you can use it also as a regular cookbook to give you special ideas. For instance, what would be a spectacular dessert that's easy to do? How

about Vesuvial Bananas? That's where the bananas are simmered in orange butter and flamed in rum. Most everyone loves a flambéed finish and this, in the Soup for Supper menu, is a snap as well as a sizzle. Or would you like a fairly plain salad to go with your otherwise quite elaborate menu? Try the pretty Salad Mimosa, where nicely dressed large lettuce leaves are sprinkled with sieved hard-boiled eggs, simple indeed but always effective. On the other hand, an imaginative and unusual salad would certainly perk up your rather drearily "healthy" main course. Start them off with a Cobb salad, that now classic tossing up of greens, crumbled Roquefort and crisp bacon, diced avocado, chicken breast, and other delicacies; you don't have to put in every item the recipe suggests when serving it as a first course.

To help you further, each menu is filled with handsome color photographs of raw ingredients as well as the cooked dishes. Generous how-to shots show you exactly how to form a tart shell, how to make noodles, how to peel the stems of broccoli, and even how to take the temperature of your soufflé! You'll find lots of good ideas here, and if you enjoy cooking and entertaining you should have a good time with these menus and recipes — and you certainly will delight your friends.

Bon Appétit!
Julia Child
1998

○ *indicates stop here*
▼ *indicates further discussion under Remarks*

Julia's Breakfasts, Lunches, and Suppers

Your own sausage and scrapple, and a home-made muffin worthy of eggs Benedict, a noble dish whose true tale now stands revealed. And other contributions to Joy in the Morning!

Breakfast Party

Menu

Eggs Benedict, with Homemade English Muffins and Three Ways of Poaching Eggs

❦

Corned Beef Hash

❦

Sautéed Chicken Livers

❦

Sour Cream and Bread Crumb Flapjacks

❦

Scrapple

❦

Homemade Sausage Cakes

❦

Fresh Fruit

❦

Milk, Fruit Juices, and Bloody Marys

There are reasons, and then there are excuses. The excuses for being festive at breakfast time (whatever that is at your house) can be anything—a football game to follow, perhaps. For me the best of all reasons is that it's an occasion to serve that beloved combination, eggs Benedict: an easy dish to mass-produce, yet one that everyone considers a special treat. It's an American dish, quite different from the French *oeufs à la Bénédictine* (a tartlet lined with *brandade de morue*—a garlicky purée of salt cod—which is surmounted by a poached egg and napped with a creamy sauce). I had understood that it was originated at the New York Yacht Club by Commodore E. C. Benedict. However, a recent check with the club's librarian, Sohei Hohri, and with Mrs. Allan Butler of Vineyard Haven, Massachusetts, has set the record straight. It seems it wasn't Mr. Benedict (who wasn't commodore at the N.Y.Y.C., but somewhere else), but his cousin Mrs. LeGrand Benedict, Mrs. Butler's great-aunt, who invented the dish; and the place wasn't the N.Y.Y.C. but Delmonico's, an elegant place to lunch at the turn of the century. Mrs. Benedict, bored with the luncheon menu, asked the maître d'hôtel to suggest something new; he asked her if she had any ideas... and, just like that, she said, "What if you put a slice of ham on half an English muffin, and a poached egg on the ham, and hollandaise sauce on the egg, and truffles on top?" And lo, a star was born.

Honor, then, to our benefactress Mrs. Benedict; and honor, too, to the butter-loving British. The object of the English muffin is to be a butter mop, and that's why it is so honeycombed with little holes, or butter wells. The recipe I use is for something between a muffin and a crumpet—cruffin? mumpet?; it is baked in rings on a griddle and made of a very spongy yeast batter, not a dough. Since I am not about to get up at 3 a.m. to cook breakfast, I make my muffins days or weeks in advance. And, when I do make them, I mix the batter the night before and let it rise once, then stir it down and often give it a second rising in the refrigerator, where it can await my pleasure. Coming down next morning, I find a swollen, adhesive, bubbly mass that looks uncannily alive. And the little yeast plants are alive, of course, and lively, because they have been gorging on starch all night. As soon as one scoops up this mass and drops it into the baking rings, set on their hot griddle, the batter becomes excited by the heat. Bubbles form at the bottom, rise upward, and seem to wink as they burst on the surface, leaving behind them little vertical wells. So graphic is this illustration of the vigor of yeast that it might give pause to believers in the transmigration of souls, the "Don't swat that fly, it might be Grandma" people.

It's nice to have the poached eggs already cooked, ready to be reheated in warm water, so famished guests can fall to at once; but what if they want seconds? Let those who want to poach them make their own. Why not? And if you have a flameproof glass saucepan, let them try the old-fashioned whirlpool method, so that they can crouch down to observe the process: the yolk twirling in its veil of white, trapped in the cone-shaped vortex. Some might want their second eggs with different underpinnings, so have some scrapple or fresh pork sausage waiting, and/or some crusty corned beef hash or sausage cakes, and a bowl of fresh tomato sauce or warm chili sauce or ketchup to splosh on top. Or perhaps they'd enjoy eggs Henriette, so have some sautéed chicken livers ready too. And stacks of pancakes, with hot butter and maybe syrup or honey to slather on.

If you have room in your kitchen, it's a great place to give this kind of party. We like to eat right there, at the big table where the morning sun falls brightest, so we set out our cold offerings on the counter tops: pitchers of milk and of orange and tomato juice—with the Bloody Mary pitcher clearly distinguished so that guests who feel fragile in the morning won't get any untoward surprise—and a great bowl of the loveliest fresh fruit we can find. From the warming drawer we bring forth platters of homemade doughnuts and coffee cake or Danish pastry. And the stove, or part of it, becomes our hot table. The bowls of chicken livers and of warm sauce are set in water-filled shallow roasting pans over low heat; platters sit on cake tins, also full of water to keep them warm; and that still leaves us a burner or two for poached egg experiments.

Right on the table we set two cozy little warming lamps, over which go two fat pots, one of strong fresh coffee and one of our favorite China tea. Made our way—we carefully measure out both boiling water and tea, and brew it in a stainless-steel pan, then strain it through a very clean stainless-steel sieve into our teapot—it keeps perfectly for hours. And it will have to. Guests at this comfortable meal will eat to bursting and then stay around to chat drowsily cuddling their warm mugs, until it's practically sunset. Don't say I didn't warn you!

Preparations

Recommended Equipment:
For homemade English muffins, you will need muffin rings, crumpet rings, or shallow tin cans with the tops and bottoms removed, and a griddle or heavy frying pan. See recipe for details.

For the other dishes, all kinds of makeshifts will work. Be sure to check out the recipe for poached eggs in advance, as various methods depend on various gadgets.

Marketing and Storage:
Staples to have on hand

Salt

Peppercorns

Herbs and spices: dried sage, oregano, thyme, tarragon; paprika, mace, and allspice

Double-acting baking powder

White vinegar or cider vinegar

Olive oil or cooking oil

Chicken bouillon and/or meat bouillon (see recipes for Corned Beef Hash, Sautéed Chicken Livers, and Scrapple for kinds and quantities)

Flour, butter, and eggs (see recipes for quantities needed)

Milk

Parsley

Fruit juices to your taste

Coffee and/or tea to your taste

Specific ingredients for this menu
All ingredients calculated for 6 people unless otherwise indicated in recipes

For Homemade English Muffins:
Dry active yeast (1 Tb)
Instant mashed potatoes (2 Tb) or raw potatoes (1)

For Eggs Benedict:
> Sliced boiled ham (about
> ½ pound or 225 g)
> English muffins (6) ▼
> Lemons (1)

For Corned Beef Hash:
> Cooked corned beef (4 cups or 2 pounds
> or 1 kg), preferably homemade
> (see page 84)
> "Boiling" or all-purpose potatoes (6 to 8)
> Onions (3 or 4)
> (Optional: heavy cream (½ cup or 1 dL)
> Fresh tomato sauce (see page 89) or chili
> sauce or ketchup

For Sautéed Chicken Livers:
> Chicken livers (1 pound or 450 g)
> Optional: fresh mushrooms (½ pound
> or 225 g)
> Port, Madeira, or dry white French ver-
> mouth

For Sour Cream and Bread Crumb Flapjacks:
> Nonsweet white bread (to make 1 cup or
> ¼ L crumbs)
> Wondra or instant-blending flour (½ cup
> or 70 g)
> Sour cream (½ cup or 1 dL)
> Syrup, honey, or whatever you fancy

For Scrapple:
> Sausage meat (4 cups or 1 L),
> preferably homemade (see page 15)
> Yellow cornmeal (1 cup or ¼ L),
> preferably stone ground
> Fragrant leaf sage

For Fresh Sausage Meat:
> Fresh ground pork (8 cups or 2 L)
> Dry white wine or vermouth

Fresh fruits in season

Optional: Assorted coffee cakes, doughnuts,
> and/or Danish pastry

▶ *Remarks:*

English muffins: Let's not be muffin snobs;
storebought are excellent. Homemade are,
simply, something else.

Homemade English Muffins

For 10 to 12 muffins

---

1 Tb dry active yeast dissolved in ¼ cup
(½ dL) tepid water

---

2 Tb instant mashed potatoes softened in ½
cup (1 dL) boiling water (or ¼ cup or ½ dL
grated raw potato simmered until tender in 1
cup or ¼ L water)

½ cup (1 dL) cold water (or cold milk if using
raw potato)

2½ cups (6 dL) all-purpose flour in a 3-quart
(3-L) mixing bowl

To be added after first rise: 1½ tsp salt dissolved in 3 Tb tepid water

---

2 to 3 Tb butter, softened

Equipment

A heavy griddle or large frying pan, or a nonstick electric skillet; muffin or crumpet rings or
cat-food or tuna-fish cans about 3 inches (8 cm)
in diameter with tops and bottoms removed; a
4- to 5-Tb ladle or long-handled cup; spatulas
(both rubber and metal); and, perhaps, pliers

---

*Pikelets (top left). Oven-baked muffins (top right).
Crumpet-muffins (bottom).*

The dough

While yeast is dissolving, assemble the other ingredients. Then into the instant potatoes beat the cold milk, and stir it along with the water and dissolved yeast into the flour. (Or, if using raw potato, stir the cold milk into the potato pan, then stir both into the flour, adding dissolved yeast only after mixture has cooled to tepid.) Beat vigorously for a minute or so with a wooden spoon to make a smooth loose thick batter, heavier than the usual pancake batter but not at all like the conventional dough. Cover with plastic wrap and let rise, preferably at around 80°F/27°C, until batter has risen and large bubbles have appeared in the surface (usually about 1½ hours—it must be bubbly, however long it takes).

Stir the batter down, then beat in the salt and water, beating vigorously for a minute. Cover and let rise until bubbles again appear in the surface—about an hour at 80°F/27°C. The batter is now ready to become English muffins.

🕐 Batter may sit for an hour or more after its second rise, or you may use one of the delaying tactics suggested at the end of the recipe.

Preliminaries to cooking the muffins

When you are ready to cook the muffins, brush insides of rings or tins fairly generously with butter; butter surface of griddle or frying pan lightly and set over moderate heat. When just hot enough so that drops of water begin to dance on it, the heat is about right. Scoop your ladle or cup into the batter and dislodge the batter into a ring or tin with rubber spatula; batter should be about ⅜ inch (1 cm) thick to make a raised muffin twice that. (Batter should be heavy, sticky, sluggish, but not runny, having just enough looseness to be spread out into the ring—if you think it is too thick, beat in tepid water by driblets.)

Cooking the muffins

The muffins are to cook slowly on one side until bubbles, which form near the bottom of the muffin, pierce through the top surface, and until almost the entire top changes from a wet ivory white to a dryish gray color; this will take 6 to 8 minutes or more, depending on the heat. (Regulate heat so that bottoms of muffins do not color more than a medium or pale brown.) Now the muffins are to be turned over for a brief cooking on the other side, and at

Batter on left has risen.

this point you can probably lift the rings off them; if not, turn them over and dislodge rings with the point of a knife, cutting and poking around the edge of rings if necessary. Cans are sometimes more difficult to remove; you may find it useful to have a pair of pliers for lifting, as well as a small knife for poking. Less than a minute is usually enough for cooking the second side, which needs only a token browning and drying out. Cool the muffins on a rack.

🕐 Fresh but cold muffins freeze beautifully and keep freshest when stored frozen, although they will stay fresh enough wrapped airtight in a plastic bag for a day or two in the refrigerator.

To serve English muffins
The muffins must be split (not cut) in half horizontally, since the inside texture should be slightly rough and full of holes (the bottoms are always solid, however). To split them, you can use a table fork, pushing the tines into the muffin all around the circumference, then gently tearing the two halves apart. Or use a serrated knife, cutting a slit in one side, then tearing the muffin apart all around and inside, using short slashes made with the point and top ½ inch (1½ cm) of the knife.

An electric toaster is not at all suitable for homemade English muffins: since the muffins are damp in texture they must be toasted very slowly under a broiler; the slow browning dries out the interior while crusting the surface. Toast the uncut side a minute or so, then turn and toast the cut side for 2 to 3 minutes, until lightly browned. Butter the cut side and return under the broiler for a moment to let the butter bubble up and sink in. Serve as soon as possible.

Remarks:
Delaying tactics and sourdough: Not much can happen to ruin this dough, as long as you have achieved the necessary bubbles. You may let it wait at room temperature for an hour or more before baking; or you may even refrigerate it overnight. If it seems to have lost its bubble, you can bring it back to life by beating in another cup of flour blended with enough tepid water to make a batter; this will give the yeast something more to feed on and in an hour or so it will rise and bubble again as it gobbles its new food.

You can even turn this batter into a sourdough. Simply let it sit at room temperature for a day or two until it has soured, then bottle and refrigerate it. You can now use it in any sourdough recipe, or you can make sourdough English muffins: blend ½ cup of it with 1 cup flour and enough water to make a batter, add 1 tablespoon dissolved yeast, and let it rise; then beat in more flour and water, or milk, and add salt (proportions make no difference as long as you get your bubbles); let it rise and bubble again; and cook your muffins. Replenish the sourdough starter by mixing it with more flour and water or milk blended into a batter, and let sit at room temperature until it has bubbled up and subsided; refrigerate as before.

To Poach an Egg

Here are three ways to poach eggs in water—and I am not talking about the electric poacher, which is really a steamer. If you are lucky enough to have very fresh eggs very recently out of the hen, you will have no trouble whatsoever; you simply break the egg into a pan of barely simmering water and in a few minutes you have the most beautiful neat perfect oval of a poached egg, the yolk cozily masked by the white all over. It is when you have store-bought eggs of uncertain date that you can at times run into exposed yolks, wispy whites, and quite unpresentable results that can be served only under a thick disguise.

However, when your eggs are reasonably fresh you can do very well as follows:
The 10-second firm-up: First prick the large end of each egg with a pin or an egg pricker, going down ¼ inch (¾ cm) into the egg; this will let the air from the pocket in the large end escape in the hot water, and prevent a burst of white from coming out of any crack in the shell. Then lower the eggs, using a slotted spoon, into a pan of boiling water, boil exactly

10 seconds, and remove at once; this gives just a little cohesion to the white, but not enough to stick it to its covering membrane or shell.

The vinegar coagulant: Vinegar coagulates the surface of the white as soon as they come in contact with each other, and although vinegar does very slightly toughen the outermost surface of the white, you are wise to use it when your eggs are not newly laid. For every quart or liter of water, pour in 2½ tablespoons of white or cider vinegar.

Timing poached eggs: The perfectly poached egg, besides being attractive, has a tender white that is just set all the way through, and a yolk that is still liquid. I find that 4 minutes in barely simmering water is just right for "large" and "extra large" eggs.

I. The whirlpool poach. Choose a rather high saucepan, 6 to 7 inches (15 to 18 cm) in both diameter and depth, add water to come ⅔ the way up, bring to the boil, and pour in 2½ tablespoons vinegar per quart or liter. Prick the eggs and boil 10 seconds in the shell. Then stir the water with a wooden spoon or spatula, going round and round the edge of the pan to create a whirlpool; quickly break an egg into the center or vortex and the swirling water

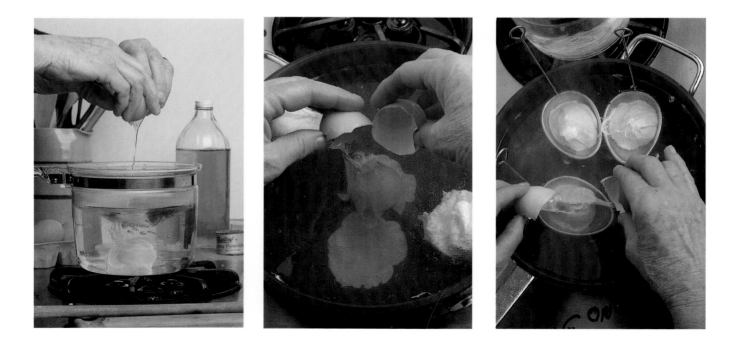

should form the egg neatly. Leave at the barest simmer for 4 minutes, then remove with a slotted spoon to a bowl of cold water.

II. The free-form free-floating egg. This is a neat trick when it works, and makes the cook feel clever. Fill a wide shallow saucepan with 1½ inches (4 cm) of water, adding the required 2½ tablespoons vinegar per quart or liter. Then, with water at the barest simmer, crack an egg and, holding it very close to the water, your fingers all but in it, swing the shell open and let the egg drop in. If you are lucky, it will form into a quite neat oval, but you can often help it, if help it needs, by rapidly rolling it over and over with a wooden spoon before it has coagulated. Set timer for 4 minutes and continue with the rest of the eggs, adding 4 to 6 in all, depending on the size of your pan; for accurate timing, start the first egg at the handle side of the pan, and move around clockwise, taking out the first egg as the timer goes off, then the second, and so forth, dropping each as it is done into a bowl of cold water.

III. The oval egg holder triumph. A most satisfactory solution to egg poaching and one which produces a handsomely shaped egg is the oval metal egg poacher with perforated bottom. (Before each poaching session, be sure to wash and wipe carefully to remove any rust or dirt in the holes.) Place the poachers in 2 inches (5 cm) of water, and proceed exactly as in the preceding directions, dropping the eggs one by one into the poachers. When your 4 minutes are up, remove the poachers one by one and very gently scoop the egg out with a dessert spoon into a bowl of cold water.

Storing poached eggs. Refrigerate poached eggs in a bowl with enough cold water to submerge them completely, but do not cover the bowl. They will keep perfectly for 2 or 3 days.

To reheat cold poached eggs. Drop into a pan of barely simmering salted water and leave for 2 minutes, then remove with a slotted spoon, and roll against a folded towel to dry them.

Eggs Benedict

For 12 eggs, 2 per serving

12 toasted and buttered English muffin halves (recipe on page 6)

12 rounds of boiled ham, lightly sautéed in butter

12 beautifully poached eggs (the preceding recipe)

About 1½ cups (½ L) hollandaise sauce (the following recipe)

Optional topping: <u>Either</u> slices of truffle <u>or</u> 1 hard-boiled egg, chopped, tossed with 3 Tb minced fresh parsley, 2 Tb minced cooked ham, and salt and pepper

Just before serving, place 2 hot toasted muffin halves on each plate and top each with a piece of ham. Heat the eggs as described in their recipe and rapidly remove from hot water with a slotted spoon, rolling each against a folded towel as you do so. Set an egg on each ham-topped muffin, spoon over a good dollop of hollandaise, and lay a slice or sprinkle on a big pinch of the optional topping. Serve at once.

A Light Hollandaise Sauce

For about 1 ½ cups

3 Tb fresh lemon juice and 3 Tb water in a small saucepan
½ tsp salt
1 whole egg and 2 yolks in a smallish stainless-steel saucepan
6 to 8 ounces (180 to 225 g) warm but not bubbling-hot butter in a small saucepan
Salt, pepper, and more lemon juice to taste

Shortly before serving, bring the lemon juice and water to the simmer, adding the salt. Meanwhile, vigorously beat the egg and yolks in their pan with a wire whip for a minute or so until they are pale and thick. Then set the yolk mixture over moderately low heat and whisk in the hot lemon juice by driblets. Continue whisking, not too fast but reaching all over bottom and corners of pan, until you have a foamy warm mass; remove from heat just as you see a wisp of steam rising. (Do not overheat or you will coagulate the egg yolks.) Immediately start beating in the warm butter by driblets, to make a thick, creamy, light, yellow sauce. Taste carefully for seasoning, adding salt, pepper, and more lemon juice to taste.

🕐 This is such an easy sauce to make that I think it best done at the last moment. Otherwise I would suggest a regular hollandaise, and if it must wait and stay warm for any length of time, beat into it 2 tablespoons of *béchamel* (white) sauce for every 2 cups or ½ liter of hollandaise; this will help to hold it. However, any egg yolk and butter sauce can be kept only warm, not hot, or it will curdle; and remember that sauces with egg yolks are prime breeding grounds for sick-making bacteria. I would therefore not hold such a sauce longer than an hour, and would prefer to make fresh sauces as often as needed rather than risk the slightest chance of food poisoning.

Corned Beef Hash

To serve 6 to 8 people

Timing note: A good hash takes at least 40 minutes to make since it must have time to crust on the bottom, and that crust is stirred into the hash several times before the final crust is formed.

2½ cups (6 dL) minced onions

2 Tb or more butter

2 Tb or more olive oil or cooking oil

3 Tb flour

¾ cup (1¾ dL) or more bouillon (cooking liquid) from the corned beef, or chicken or beef broth

4 cups or more diced boiled potatoes (I like "boiling" or all-purpose potatoes because they keep their shape during cooking)

4 cups or more chopped or roughly ground cooked corned beef

½ tsp or so minced herbs such as sage, oregano, thyme, or a mixture

5 to 6 Tb or so minced fresh parsley

Salt and pepper

½ cup (1 dL) or so heavy cream (optional)

Equipment

A heavy frying pan or electric skillet with cover, 12 inches (30 cm) top diameter, and if you plan to unmold the hash it should be of well-seasoned iron or have a nonstick surface; an oiled pizza pan also, if you plan to unmold

The hash mixture

Sauté the onions slowly in 2 Tb each butter and oil for 6 to 8 minutes, stirring frequently, until tender, then raise heat slightly and let them brown a bit. Lower heat again; blend in the flour and a little more butter or oil if needed to make a paste; stir and cook slowly for 2 minutes. Blend in ¾ cup (1¾ dL) bouil-lon or broth, let boil a moment, then mix in the potatoes, corned beef, herbs, and parsley. Taste carefully for seasoning, and if hash seems dry blend in tablespoons of optional cream or more bouillon.

Cooking the hash

Rather firmly, press the hash down all over with the flat of a spatula, set a cover over the pan, and cook slowly for about 15 minutes or until the hash has crusted on the bottom. Stir it up to mix some of the crust into the body of the hash, and repeat the process, being careful not to overcook and dry it out (or it will not be cohesive enough to unmold properly). Taste and correct seasoning.

🕐 Hash may be cooked in advance to this point; set aside off heat, and you may cover and refrigerate it when cold. Reheat slowly, covered, then proceed.

Some 10 to 15 minutes before serving, uncover the hash, press it down all over with a spatula, and let it form its final crust over moderate heat.

Serving

You may serve the hash as is, turning each serving upside down on the plate to present a crusted surface. Or you may wish to unmold it in a half-moon shape onto a platter: to do so, start sliding the large cake of hash onto a hot platter but stop at the halfway mark, then, holding pan by its handle, your thumb underneath, quickly flip pan upside down to turn other half of hash neatly over the first, crusted bottom in full view. (This can often be a tricky business, but it does help to have the first half of the hash thinner than the other half and a small pan is far easier to control than the large one described here.) A second unmolding system is to slide the whole cake of hash out onto an oiled pizza tray; then turn the frying pan or a round platter upside down over it and reverse the two, leaving the hash crusted side up. In either case, cracks and musses can be hidden under a sprinkling of chopped parsley.

Accompaniments

Serve each helping of hash with a fried or poached egg on top, and a dollop of fresh tomato sauce or of warm ketchup or chili sauce.

Sautéed Chicken Livers

For 6 to 8 small servings

1 pound (450 g) chicken livers

Salt, pepper, and flour

2 Tb butter and 1 of oil (more if needed)

About ½ cup (1 dL) chicken stock or broth (more if needed)

4 Tb Port, Madeira, or dry white French vermouth

A sprinkling of tarragon (optional)

½ pound (225 g) fresh mushrooms, quartered and sautéed separately in butter (optional)

1 Tb or more butter as final enrichment (optional)

2 to 3 Tb fresh minced parsley

To prepare the livers for cooking, look them over to be sure no black or greenish bile spots are on the surface. If so, shave them off since they are bitter; although this is a rare occurrence, it is well to watch for it. Just before sautéing, dry the livers in paper towels; then place on wax paper and toss with a sprinkling of salt and pepper, and then of flour, to give them a light dusting. Immediately, then, get to the sautéing: set a heavy 10-inch (25-cm) frying pan over high heat, add to it enough butter to film the bottom, plus ½ that amount of oil. When the butter foam begins to subside, toss in as many livers as will fit in one layer. Turn and toss for 2 to 3 minutes until, when you press them, the livers have changed from squashy raw to just resistant to your finger. Pour in the stock and wine, the optional tarragon and mushrooms, and boil rapidly, tossing and turning the livers for a moment or two until liquid thickens lightly. Taste and correct seasoning.

🕐 May be cooked in advance; set aside uncovered.

Just before serving toss over moderately high heat, adding more liquid if you feel it necessary, a tablespoon or so of butter if you wish, and the parsley.

Sour Cream and Bread Crumb Flapjacks

Tender pancakes

For about 10 pancakes 4 inches in diameter

1 cup (¼ L) toasted fresh, nonsweet white bread crumbs

4 Tb melted butter

1 egg

½ cup (1 dL) Wondra or instant-blending flour

½ cup (1 dL) sour cream

½ cup (1 dL) or more milk

½ tsp double-acting baking powder

Salt and pepper

To make toasted bread crumbs, crumb fresh bread in a blender or processor, then spread out in a roasting pan in a preheated 350°F/180°C oven, and toss until lightly browned—15 to 20 minutes. Toss in a frying pan with the melted butter over moderate heat.

Blend egg, flour, sour cream, ½ cup (1 dL) milk, and baking powder in a 4-cup (1-L) measure; fold in the buttered crumbs and salt and pepper to taste. Stir in driblets more milk if you think it necessary (but can you tell until you have tried a pancake?).

Drop batter onto a buttered hot skillet and cook pancakes, turning when bubbles appear on the surface.

Serve with melted butter and maple syrup or honey.

Scrapple

*For an 8-cup loaf pan, serving 12
or more*

4 cups (1 L) sausage meat, preferably homemade (see recipe following)
4 cups (1 L) pork stock or other flavorful meat stock in a 3-quart (3-L) saucepan with heavy bottom
1 Tb or more fragrant leaf sage
1 cup (225 g) yellow cornmeal, stone ground preferred
½ cup (1 dL) cold water
3 eggs
Salt and pepper
Equipment
An 8-cup (2-L) loaf pan or baking dish, and a board or plate that will fit into it for weighting down scrapple after baking

Sauté sausage meat in a large frying pan until it turns from pink to gray, breaking it up with a fork as you do so—5 minutes or more. Drain in a sieve set over a bowl, and reserve fat—which may be used for sautéing finished scrapple later.

Meanwhile, bring the stock to the boil, adding sage to taste. Mix the cornmeal with the cold water in a bowl, then whisk in a cupful of the hot stock. Return cornmeal to stock, bring to the boil whisking slowly, and cook for 5 minutes or more until mixture is thick, like cornmeal mush. Cover pan, set in a larger pan of simmering water, and cook for 30 minutes. Remove from pan of hot water and boil over moderately high heat, stirring with a wooden spoon, until cornmeal is thick and heavy and holds its shape in a spoon—the thicker the better, so that it will unmold and slice easily later.

Beat the cooked and drained sausage meat into the cornmeal, breaking it up so that it will blend nicely, and boil, stirring and beating, for 3 to 4 minutes. Beat in the eggs. Taste carefully for seasoning: scrapple is traditionally fragrant with sage and highly seasoned.

Butter an 8-cup (2-L) loaf pan, line bottom of pan with wax paper, and turn the cornmeal mixture into it. Cover with wax paper and aluminum foil and bake for an hour or more in a preheated 350°F/180°C oven, until mixture has swelled and is bubbling hot.

Remove from oven, place a board on top of the scrapple (over the wax paper and foil) and a 5-pound (2¼-kg) weight (canned goods, meat grinder, etc.), and let cool. When cold, remove weight and board, cover airtight, and chill.

🕐 Once baked in its pan, scrapple will keep for at least 2 to 3 weeks in the refrigerator. It can be frozen; however, pork products tend to lose texture and savor after 2 months or so in the freezer.

To serve, run a knife around inside of mold, then set mold on top of stove to heat and loosen bottom; unmold onto a cutting board. Slice into serving pieces about ⅜ inch (1 cm) thick. Dredge lightly in cornmeal, and brown on both sides in rendered sausage fat or butter.

Serve for breakfast with fried or poached eggs, or fried apple slices; or use as a dinner meat, accompanying the scrapple with green vegetables such as broccoli or cabbage, or a green salad, or cole slaw.

Remarks:

Traditional farm scrapple is made, literally, from pork scraps and bones that are boiled up together for 2 hours or so with herbs and aromatic vegetables—carrots, onions, celery. The meat adhering to the bones is then scraped off and chopped, along with the other pork meat scraps. The cooking broth is strained and boiled up with the cornmeal, then the two are combined, and that is the scrapple. If you have cured your own pork, as in the recipe on page 84, you can use the same system whether you decide to bone your pork before or after salting (and soaking) it. Once you have chopped the boiled meat, you can substitute it for the sausage in the preceding recipe. Simply stir it into the saucepan of cooked cornmeal, which has been boiled up with your pork-cooking liquid, and continue with the recipe.

Fresh Sausage Meat

For about 8 cups, or 4 pounds

8 cups (2 L) fresh ground pork—including 2 to 3 cups (½ to ¾ L) fresh pork fat or blanched salt pork fat—from shoulder, rib, or loin
1 Tb salt
1 Tb sage
1 tsp mace
½ tsp cracked pepper
1 tsp paprika
4 to 5 Tb white wine or vermouth
Optional other herbs: thyme, allspice

Grind pork not too fine in meat grinder or processor, beating in seasonings and wine or vermouth (to lighten the mixture). Sauté a spoonful and taste, then correct seasoning as you feel necessary.

🕐 Best made a day ahead, so that flavoring will have time to blend with meat.

To be used in the preceding scrapple, or to sauté in cakes, as breakfast sausage.

Scrapple made from fresh cornmeal and fresh sausage meat surrounding a platter of scrambled eggs

🕐 Timing

Because breakfast is such a personal meal, this chapter offers you a choice of dishes from which you might like to compose your own menu. Supposing, however, that you want to take on the whole shooting match, the work could be divided up as follows:

During the party, cook pancakes and assemble eggs Benedict to order. This means having on hand a pitcher of pancake batter, a bowl of warm water (to reheat the eggs), hot toasted and buttered muffins, hot sautéed ham slices, and warm hollandaise sauce. You can prepare all of these half an hour in advance.

Scrapple, too, is fried to order, or fried just beforehand and kept warm; and the same goes for the sausage cakes.

Corned beef hash takes about 45 minutes (with some attention from you) to form a good crust; it may be kept warm over hot water. You could cook it till not quite done the night before, cool and refrigerate, and finish the crust 10 minutes before the party.

Eggs may be poached up to 2 or 3 days in advance and kept refrigerated, uncovered, in a bowl of water.

Muffins freeze perfectly; you can wait until that morning to thaw, split, toast, butter, and toast again.

Coffee and tea must be made that morning, but will keep over low heat if you don't let them get cold—or scalded—at any time.

Corned beef keeps almost indefinitely; sausage meat and scrapple can stay in the freezer for up to 2 months.

Menu Variations

English muffins: See the Postscript to this chapter for other kinds of yeast batter griddle cakes. And I need not remind you that the English muffin, known in my youth as the Garbo, can get away with almost anything, including peanut butter. Peanut Garbos! Divine.

Eggs Benedict: You can substitute Canadian bacon for the ham, and toast or little pastry cases for the muffins. Keeping only the poached egg, you can switch everything else around: with chicken livers, it's an egg Henriette; with spinach, an egg Florentine; you can sit it on a sliced grilled tomato; you can use cheese sauce (eggs à la Mornay), or tomato sauce, or a *soubise....* Escoffier has some 19 recipes, all with resounding names.

Corned beef hash: See page 84 for how to corn pork, and try hashing that. Or add beets for red flannel hash. Or cook it in little cakes; it doesn't have to be a big pillow. Or hash leftover chicken or turkey, going a bit lighter on the seasoning and adding cream. Or hash lamb, perhaps adding cooked rice or kasha instead of potatoes.

Chicken livers: You could broil them on skewers instead of sautéing them, or use duck or other poultry livers if you like a stronger flavor. Chopped fine, combined with mushroom *duxelles,* quickly sautéed and moistened with a little leftover gravy flavored with Port or Madeira, they make a luxurious spread for hot buttered toast. Thinly sliced sautéed calf's liver is also nice with eggs for a hearty breakfast.

Pancakes: These are fairly close cousins to the muffin variants in the Postscript—to pikelets in particular. You can bake almost any batter on a griddle (buckwheat, rye, oat, barley, corn, etc.), and don't forget the charm of grated potato pancakes blobbed with sour cream, or mashed-potato pancakes. Or lovely yeasty blini, nice with smoked fish as well as with caviar—nice with butter and honey, for that matter. Or Swedish pancakes, maybe with lingonberries. Or French crêpes, rolled around a creamed mixture and sauced, or, especially for children, rolled around a spoonful of jam and dusted with confectioners sugar. Or palatschinken, or tortillas, or . . . well, every nation has its pancakes.

Scrapple: You can eat it with fried tomato or apple slices; you can use pork liver and other scraps in the recipe; you can use oatmeal instead of cornmeal (in which case it's called "goetta")—but I can't really think of any variations in cooking it.

Sausage meat: For other sausage makings, check out *Mastering II* and *J.C.'s Kitchen.* And sometime try baking homemade sausage in a pastry crust.

Grated potato pancakes and sausages waiting for their blob of sour cream

Leftovers

Poached eggs: If you have extra ones, even rewarmed, congratulations. Coat them with aspic for eggs *en gelée*—an exquisite cold appetizer. Warm them, then sauce and bed them with and on practically anything. Tuck them into a soufflé, bedded on about ⅓ of the mixture, then covered with the rest. *Ham:* I don't need to suggest what to do with extra sliced ham. *Muffins:* If you have some unsplit, they freeze (or refreeze) perfectly. *Hollandaise sauce:* If it has sat around long, I don't think it's safe to keep. If it hasn't, you can refrigerate and rewarm cautiously to tepid.

Hash and *scrapple:* Chill or refreeze any uncooked leftovers. And do likewise with uncooked *sausage meat*, although this you can combine with other meats, in meatballs, in hamburgers, and in terrines and *pâtés*.

Chicken livers: Once they're cooked, I'd make them into a simple *pâté*—you can just run them through a processor or blender with a little cream and beat into softened butter, then chill.

Pancakes: Leftover cooked pancakes will freeze but, because it contains baking powder, the batter won't keep. However, if it's still fairly lively you could stir in enough flour to make a light dough, and bake in muffin tins.

Postscript: More on muffins

Remember the schoolbook story of how King Alfred let the poor cottager's cakes burn as he sat by the hearth worrying about the Danish invaders? Even back in the 800s, those "cakes" were probably muffins and probably made with yeast, which has been known since the dawn of history.

Most home cooks in France, where I got my culinary education, never learn bread making at all, so I came late to its ancient mysteries, which still give me a sense of awe—a sense shared, and poetically expressed, by Elizabeth David. If you too are fascinated, I refer you to her masterly account of British baking, *English Bread and Yeast Cookery* (London: Penguin Books, 1978).

Apropos muffins and crumpets, Mrs. David says, in a whole chapter devoted to them, that the distinction is rather foggy and the batter similar; but the crumpet is only half as thick and holds more butter because you don't split it. The same combination of yeast batter and griddle cooking (using all kinds of flours) gives you the pikelet (baked without a ring, flat and free-form), the girdle cake, the bannock, and the scone of Scotland. The latter two may be baked in the oven, as is the plump Scottish bap. Mrs. David says that many country kitchens in the British Isles still keep their ancient bake stones and baking irons, used right in the hearth. King Alfred would feel right at home.

For unspecified numbers, at unpredictable hours, a festive but practical menu. One of its minor components is the Perfectly Peelable HB Egg, on which there is new news.

Holiday Lunch

Menu

Chicken Melon, or Poulet de Charente à la Melonaise
Rosie's Great Potato Salad
Mayonnaise in the Food Processor
Skewered Vegetable Salad
Boston or Butter Lettuce Salad

ॐ

Apple Turnover

ॐ

Suggested wines:
Beaujolais, Côtes du Rhône, Zinfandel, or a very good rosé

The thing is, we'd forgotten tomorrow was a holiday when we started asking people to lunch. Naturally it turned out they all were expecting houseguests, or children back from college with friends and about four sets of plans apiece. "See, Ma, if Johnny can get his clutch fixed he'll give us a ride back, but if he can't we'll have to take the two o'clock if you could just give us a lift over" kind of thing. Of course I said to the distracted ma's, "Well, come when you can, and bring whom you please," and thought no more about it until yesterday, when Paul pointed out that what we propose to do is feed lunch to anywhere from 6 to 20 guests, any time from noon until three.

It therefore follows, with cast-iron logic, that I am now doing funny things with chickens. Like most cooks, I tot up the limitations first, then look at the remaining possibilities. Six to 20 guests may mean huge leftovers; mustn't waste. We blew ourselves to veal on Monday, so we can't spend the moon today. We want to feel free tomorrow, so we cook now. We don't know all these friends-of-friends or their tastes: what does everybody like? And what is nobody allergic to? So far, a "made dish" (as opposed to a roast or sauté) of chicken looks a good answer. *But* it can't be hot, or it would dry out in three hours; and it can't be chilled, like an aspic, because the non-melting kind is rubbery. And we want the serving platter to stay attractive while under attack during a three-hour span.

However: the possibilities. Our friend Rosie the salad whiz is visiting us. We do have our faithful food processor, and Paul says he'll shell pistachio nuts and peel apples. Most of our friends' kids, home from cafeterialand, appreciate fancy food as never before.

So, our menu. Nothing could be more classical, or classier, than chicken boned to make *pâté* and roasted to a lovely color, and it feeds a lot of people. One could do it in the traditional *ballottine* shape, like a log; but you don't need calculus to see that the optimum form, with most volume to least surface, is a sphere. So a round, melon-shaped *pâté* it will be. I'll do three, keep one in reserve, put one, uncut, in the middle of my big round platter, then slice the third and make a wreath of perfect, even sections. No carving, no mess; and, if only half the people come, I'll have another party.

It won't take the three of us long to fix this festive meal, and right now the kitchen is a hive of industry. Rosie, with an artist's eye and a potter's deft hand, is preparing the makings of her three salads, each the last word of its kind: vegetable, lettuce, and potato. Perched on a high stool with a bowl in his lap, Paul is briskly popping pistachio shells for the tiny green kernels that look so pretty and crunch so nicely in a *pâté.* Every so often he darts a glance out the window: one of the resident squirrels, extra lithe or extra smart, knows a way into the bird feeder. Sometimes we scold him, but mostly, I admit, we bribe him; and he loves pistachios. "Here, you rogue," and Paul flips one out.

I've boned and defleshed the chickens' skins and sewn each into a loose pouch. In goes the stuffing, nuts and all, while Paul starts peeling apples for the dessert. The chickens did look odd, bereft of shape; but now, tied in their cheesecloth corsets, they're firming up. Then the string: each loop, like a natural rib, reinforces the melon form. *Fathoms of string…can do most anything…* I find myself humming to "I Get a Kick Out of You," and realize suddenly that Cole Porter, as usual, got the tune right; but it took a cook to discover the real words. I have a Thing about String…

"So you have," says Rosie. "Why not decorate your turnover to look like a fat, well-tied parcel?"

Preparations

Recommended Equipment:
Knives and knife sharpening

To make Chicken Melon (see recipe), a sharp boning knife, white string, a trussing or mattress needle, and cheesecloth are essential. Especially important is the knife: if it won't cut like a razor, the boning and defleshing of a chicken are a horrendous if not impossible undertaking. You want a stout sharp-pointed knife, and I like a slightly curved 6-inch (15-cm) blade for this type of work. You should also have the proper sharpening equipment, since no knife, however fine its quality, will keep an edge—it will only take an edge. Get yourself, therefore, a proper butcher's steel, the kind with a foot-long (30-cm) rod of finely ridged steel set into a handle. To sharpen the knife, sweep its blade from its handle end to its tip down the length of the steel, holding the blade at a 20-degree angle—the movement is as though the steel were a long pencil that you were sharpening. Give a half-dozen swipes down one side, then down the other, and that should hone the blade to perfect cut-ability. For very dull knives, however, you should also have a carborundum oil stone, fine on one side and a little rougher on the other; use the same general technique first on the rough side, then on the smooth, and finish up on your butcher's steel.

Disagreement note

Some practitioners sharpen their knives in the other direction on the theory that this realigns the molecules in the steel. In my system you are pushing the steel back from the cutting edge to make it sharp. Both systems seem to work and if I have a particularly dull knife I sharpen it both ways, hoping for results.

Marketing and Storage:
Staples to have on hand
(Quantities for 6 people)

Salt
Black and white peppercorns (see Remarks, page 42)
Nutmeg
Fragrant dried tarragon
Optional: powdered cinnamon
Mustard (the strong Dijon type)
Cider vinegar and wine vinegar
Crisp dill pickles (1 small)
Canned pimiento
Chicken broth (½ cup or 1 dL)
Fresh olive, peanut, and/or salad oil ▼
Ingredients for a *vinaigrette* dressing ▼
Unsalted butter (12 ounces or 340 g)
Shortening
Heavy cream (1 cup or ¼ L ; and more if desired to accompany dessert)
Eggs (12)
All-purpose flour (unbleached preferred)
Plain bleached cake flour
Granulated sugar

Lemons (1)
Onions (1)
Celery (1 stalk)
"Boiling" potatoes (3 pounds or 1½ kg)
Shallots or scallions
Curly parsley, chives, and/or other fresh herbs
Recommended: flat-leaf parsley
Cognac

Specific ingredients for this menu
(Quantities for 6 people)

Roasting chicken or capon (6 to 7 pounds or
       2¾ to 3¼ kg) ▼
Boned and skinned chicken breast (1, or
       possibly 2) ▼
Boiled ham (¼ pound or 115 g)
Pistachio nuts (4 ounces or 115 g)
Boston or butter lettuce (2 heads)
Cooking apples (4 or 5) ▼
For the skewered salad, select among the
       following:
Artichokes
Avocados
Cherry tomatoes
Cucumbers
Mushrooms
Onions (small white)
Peppers (bell type: green, red, or both)
Potatoes (small new)
Topinambours (Jerusalem artichokes or
       sunchokes)
Turnips
Zucchini

▶ *Remarks:*
Staples
Olive, peanut, and salad oils: These may be
used singly or in combination; just be sure
your oil is fresh and of best quality.
Homemade vinaigrette dressing: See page 110
for recipe.
Ingredients for this menu
Chicken: If you don't think yours is plump
enough to supply 4 cups (1 L) ground meat
after boning, buy an additional skinless,
boneless chicken breast. *Cooking apples:* See
recipe for varieties.

Chicken Melon

*Boned and stuffed chicken formed, in its
own skin, into a pâté the shape of a
melon.*

You can perform this operation on a small
frying chicken, but it is far more impressive,
and serves far more people, when you find
yourself a large roaster or capon. In fact, there
is no reason why you could not use the same
system on a turkey—but heaven knows how
long a 20-pound (10-kilo) bird would take in
the oven. Not me! (My fanciful French title,
Poulet de Charente à la Melonaise, was
suggested by the small sweet spring melons
from the Charente district of France, plus a
corruption of *à la Milanaise,* a classical appel-
lation from the old school designating a cheesy
Italianesque concoction from the region of
Milan. Of course, this chicken contains neither
melon nor cheese, but it might describe to a
knowing gastronome some conception of the
dish. We have to have a little fun with this sort
of thing, I think!)

For 14 to 16 servings

A 6- to 7-pound (2 ¾- to 3 ¼-kg) roasting chicken or capon

For the stuffing
To make about 5 cups (1 ¼ liters)

4 cups (1 L) ground chicken meat—salvaged from the boned chicken, plus 1 or more skinless and boneless chicken-breast halves if needed

1 whole egg plus 1 egg white

1 ½ tsp salt

9 grinds of the pepper mill

2 Tb minced shallots or scallions

A big speck nutmeg

½ tsp fragrant dried tarragon

2 to 3 Tb Cognac

1 cup (¼ L) chilled heavy cream

Garniture for the stuffing

1 chicken breast, cut into ¼-inch (¾-cm) dice

⅔ cup (1 ½ dL) boiled ham, diced as above

5 Tb shelled pistachio nuts

Salt and pepper

1 Tb finely minced shallots or scallions

1 Tb Cognac

Pinch fragrant dried tarragon

Other ingredients

Salt and pepper

Drops of Cognac

Several Tb melted butter

Equipment

A very sharp boning knife; a large ball of plain white string (butcher's corned-beef twine); a trussing needle—a mattress or sail-maker's needle; a square of washed cheesecloth about 20 inches (50 cm) to a side

Boning the chicken

Your object here is to remove the carcass from the chicken leaving the skin intact except at the openings at the back vent and the neck and along the backbone. The meat of the chicken will go into your stuffing, and the skin will be the container for the *pâté* mixture. Proceed as follows.

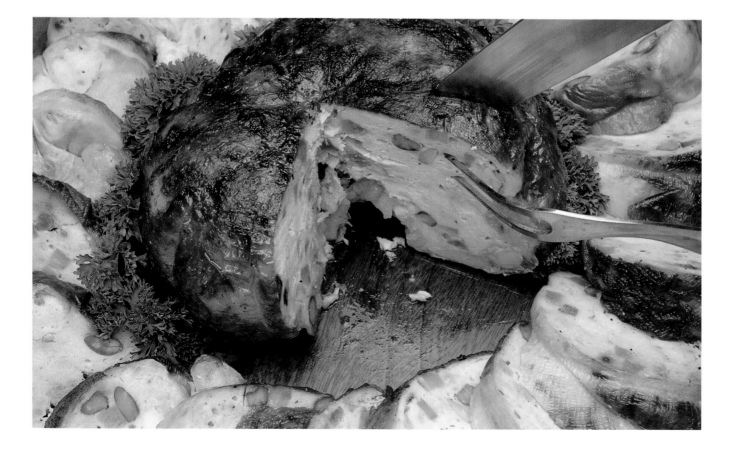

First, for easy removal of meat from skin after boning, slip your fingers between meat and skin at the neck opening, and loosen skin all around breast, thighs, and as far down the drumsticks as you can—being careful not to tear the skin.

Then turn the chicken on its side and make a slit down the backbone from neck end to tail end. One side at a time, scrape down backbone, severing ball joints of wings at shoulder and of thigh at small of back and continuing down rib cage and side of breastbone until you come near its edge, at top of breast. Stop! Skin is very thin over ridge of breastbone and easily pierced. Do the same on the other side. Finally lift carcass and scrape close under ridge of breastbone (not against skin) to free the carcass. To remove wing and leg bones easily, chop off wings above elbows and chop ball joints off ends of drumsticks. Then remove

wing, thigh, and drumstick bones from inside the chicken, poking their skin sleeves inside out onto flesh side of chicken. Carefully cut and pull as much of the meat as you can from the chicken skin without piercing it. Sprinkle inside of chicken skin with a little salt and drops of Cognac. Reserve bones and carcass for chicken stock. Dice one breast-meat half and reserve for stuffing garniture, using second breast half and rest of meat to grind up for stuffing.

↓

↓

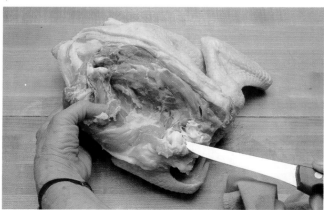

↓

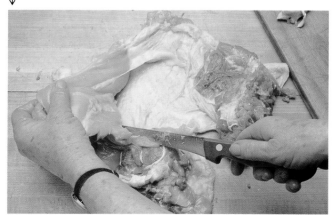

The stuffing

(If you do not have a food processor, grind up the meat, then beat in the rest of the ingredients.) Cut the meat into 1-inch (2½-cm) pieces and purée in the processor in 2 or 3 batches. Then return all to food processor, add the rest of the ingredients listed for the stuffing, and purée for a minute or so until finely ground. Sauté a spoonful in a small frying pan, taste, and add more seasoning if you think it necessary. Toss the garniture chicken, ham, pistachios, and seasonings in a bowl and let sit until you are ready to stuff the chicken, then fold into the stuffing.

Stuffing the chicken

Thread your trussing needle with a good 16 inches (40 cm) of string, and you are now ready to make a pouch, with drawstring, of the chicken skin. To do so, sew a loose basting stitch around the circumference of the chicken skin and draw up the two ends of the string slightly to make an open pouch. Fill the pouch with the stuffing (not too full), pull the string

taut, and tie. Dip the cheesecloth square into melted butter, spread out on your work surface, and place the chicken, tie side up, in the middle. Tie the 2 opposite corners of cheesecloth together over the chicken, then the other 2 ends, to enclose the chicken in a ball shape. Cut off extra cheesecloth. Then, always from the central tie, wind successive rounds of string around the ball to make the melon pattern. (Hold one end of string taut as a guideline and twist free end about it to secure each loop as you wind it around the chicken.) Chicken is now ready to roast.

🕐   May be prepared a day in advance and refrigerated; may be frozen, but thaw before roasting.

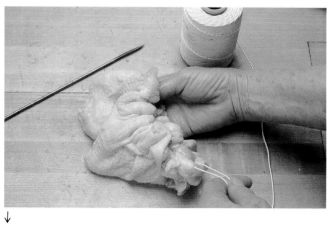

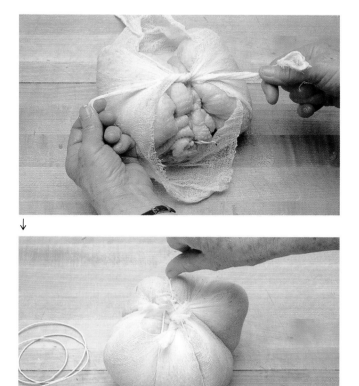

Roasting and serving
(So that chicken will brown nicely on the top as well as the bottom, but so that it will not lose its juices, start it tie side down and turn after 25 to 30 minutes, before any juices have managed to escape from that side.) Preheat oven to 350°F/180°C. Set chicken tie side down on a lightly buttered pie dish and roast in middle level of oven for 25 to 30 minutes to brown top nicely, then turn tie side up for the rest of the roasting. Baste occasionally with accumulated fat in dish. Chicken is done at a thermometer reading of 170°F/77°C. (Total cooking time is 1½ to 2 hours.) Remove and let rest 20 minutes, then carefully ease off the cheesecloth and string without tearing chicken skin.

Serve hot with pan juices and *béarnaise* sauce. Or let cool to room temperature, cover, and chill; serve as you would a *pâté,* as part of a cold lunch or as the first course for a dinner. To carve, cut into wedges, starting from the center, as though cutting a thick pie.

Rosie's Great Potato Salad

After Rosie had tried a number of off-beat combinations and additions, hoping that the best possible salad might be something un-usual, she concluded that the thing to aim at was that old-fashioned taste where the pota-toes dominate and where there is just enough onion, the right amount of celery for a bit of crunch, enough eggs for their subtle effect, plus a light but sufficient binding and melding with the best mayonnaise. Here is her recipe.

For about 2 quarts (2 liters),
serving 6 to 8

3 pounds (1½ kg) "boiling" potatoes, the type that will keep their shape when cooked and sliced—such as round red potatoes or new potatoes
½ cup (1 dL) chicken broth mixed with 2 to 3 Tb cider vinegar
Salt and pepper
1 medium-size to large mild onion, finely diced
1 medium-size stalk celery, finely diced
1 small crisp dill pickle, finely diced
3 hard-boiled eggs, diced
2 Tb minced fresh parsley, preferably the flat-leaf variety
1 canned pimiento, diced
½ to ¾ cup (1 to 1¾ dL) homemade mayon-naise (see next recipe)
For decoration
Strips of canned pimiento
Parsley and/or chives
Sliced or quartered hard-boiled eggs (see recipe at end of chapter)

Scrub the potatoes and boil in their jackets, in lightly salted water, just until tender (halve a potato and eat a slice to be sure). Then drain off water, cover pan, and let sit for 5 minutes to let them firm up and to make for easier slic-ing. Peel while still warm and cut into slices about 3/16 inch (¾ cm) thick. Toss the still-warm potatoes gently in a large mixing bowl with the broth and with salt and pepper to taste. Salt the diced onion lightly and add to the potatoes along with the celery, pickle, eggs, parsley, and pimiento. Toss and fold gently to blend flavors. Taste carefully and correct seasoning. When cool, fold in two-thirds of the mayonnaise, saving the rest for decoration.

🕐 May be made a day in advance; cover and refrigerate.

An hour or so before you are ready to serve, taste again for seasoning and turn the salad into a nice bowl; mask the top with the remaining mayonnaise and decorate with pimiento, herbs, and eggs.

Remarks:

Rosie suggests, when you are making larger quantities, that you toss the equivalent of the above ingredients in a mixing bowl (or several bowls), turn that into a larger bowl, and continue with the same amount, adding each batch as you do it to the larger bowl. This way you can easily manage the potatoes and the perfection of the seasoning without breaking the slices.

Mayonnaise in the Food Processor

Certainly the easiest way to make mayonnaise is in the food processor, where in 2 or 3 minutes you have 2 or 3 cups (or ½ liter). Regardless of method, the best mayonnaise is made from the freshest and best ingredients, since nothing can disguise a cheap-tasting oil, a harsh vinegar, or a fake lemon.

For about 2 ¼ cups (½ liter)

1 whole egg
2 egg yolks
1 tsp strong prepared mustard (Dijon type)
½ tsp or more salt
1 Tb or more fresh lemon juice or wine vinegar
2 cups best-quality light olive oil, salad oil, or fresh peanut oil—all one kind or a combination
White pepper

Using the metal blade (I never use the plastic one for anything), process the egg, yolks, mustard, and ½ teaspoon salt for 30 seconds. Then add 1 tablespoon lemon juice or vinegar and process half a minute more. Finally, in a very thin stream, pour in the oil. When all has gone in, remove cover, check consistency, and taste for seasoning: you will probably want to beat in a little more lemon juice or vinegar, and salt and white pepper, but you can also beat in driblets of cold water for a milder and lighter taste and texture.

Remarks:
The purpose of the whole egg here is to dilute the thickening capacity of the yolks, since if you have all yolks the mayonnaise stiffens so much in the machine you cannot add the full amount of oil. However, you can thin the sauce with droplets of water rather than egg white. The proportions I use are 3 yolks for every 2 cups or ½ liter of oil, and, in the processor, 1 egg white.

Turned, or thinned-out, mayonnaise:
I am not always successful with the processor when I have a badly thinned-out mayonnaise. (This sometimes happens when the mayonnaise has been kept in too cold a refrigerator: the emulsion property of the egg yolks has broken down, and they release the oil from suspension.) To restore the mayonnaise it has to be reconstituted bit by bit, and because the processor can't manage a small enough quantity initially to begin the homogenizing and reconstituting process, I've had more luck bringing the sauce back by hand or in an electric blender. I suggest that you start with a half tablespoon of Dijon-type prepared mustard and a tablespoon of thinned-out mayonnaise and beat vigorously in a bowl or blender until the mixture has thickened; then beat in the thinned-out sauce by driblets—it is the very slow addition of the sauce, particularly at first, that brings it back to its thick emulsified state.

Freezing homemade mayonnaise: It often happens to me that I've a nice jar of homemade mayonnaise in my refrigerator and then we go off somewhere on a vacation. I've found that I can freeze it, let it defrost in the refrigerator, and then reconstitute it just as though it were the thinned-out mayonnaise in the preceding paragraph.

Using frozen egg yolks for mayonnaise:
Thaw the egg yolks at room temperature or overnight in the refrigerator. Then whip them in an electric blender or food processor (if you have enough for the food processor—4 or 5 at least), adding a tablespoon of prepared mustard and another of lemon juice or vinegar, and proceed as usual.

Skewered Salad

Vegetable salad en brochettes

This attractive way to serve salad vegetables makes it easy for guests, who pick up a skewered collection and bear it off on their plates. Use any combination of cooked and raw vegetables that appeals to you and will skewer successfully. Be sure, however, to use skewers with flat sides or double prongs, or two skewers per serving; the vegetables must hang in there, and the skewer must be solid enough to stay rigid from platter to plate. I find it best to prepare each vegetable separately and then marinate it in dressing long enough for it to pick up the desired taste, but not so long as to wilt it. Green vegetables and toma- toes, for instance, can wilt, while potatoes and topinambours will thrive in a dressing. Skewer the vegetables half an hour or so before your guests arrive, arrange in a platter, cover, and refrigerate. Just before serving, spoon on a little more dressing and sprinkle on finely minced fresh herbs, such as parsley and chives, or whatever other herbal delight your garden offers, like fresh chervil, tarragon, or basil. Here are some vegetable choices that have been successfully skewered in our house. (See index for various dressings.)

Artichokes: hearts or bottoms, cooked in a *blanc* (as described on page 31 of *Julia's Casual Dinners*) and halved or quartered, depending on size. Toss in the dressing half an hour or longer before skewering.

Avocados: skewered at the last minute. However, avocado chunks will hold quite nicely if you dip them first for a moment in a solution of cold water and lemon juice, in the proportions of 1 tablespoon of lemon juice for 8 of water.

Cherry tomatoes: either impaled whole, as is, or halved and tossed in dressing just before skewering.

Cucumbers: peeled, halved lengthwise, seeded, and cut into chunks. I always marinate them first for 20 minutes or longer in a little salt, a pinch of sugar, and droplets of wine vinegar (¼ teaspoon salt, ⅛ teaspoon sugar, and ½ teaspoon vinegar per cucumber).

Mushrooms: use small caps or quartered large caps and drop for 1 minute in boiling water with lemon and salt to keep them fresh- looking. Toss in the dressing and leave for an hour, or more if you wish, before skewering.

Onions: the very small white ones. Drop into boiling water for ½ minute, then peel and simmer until just tender in lightly

salted water. Marinate for as long as you wish in the dressing.

Peppers: either green or red, halved, seeded, and cut into 1-inch (2½-cm) pieces. Drop them for 1 minute into boiling water just to soften slightly, then drain. Toss in dressing just before skewering.

Potatoes: small new ones. Boil in their skins in lightly salted water, just until tender. Peel or not, as you wish. Marinate while still warm in your dressing for as long as you like. (You wouldn't need potatoes when serving potato salad, of course, but they are good on skewers—be sure you have the waxy boiling kind or they will break up when pierced.)

Topinambours (Jerusalem artichokes or sunchokes): cook them in a *blanc* (as described on page 51 of *Julia's Casual Dinners*) and toss while still warm in the dressing, letting them marinate for as long as you wish.

Turnips: white turnips or even the yellow rutabaga. Peel, cut into appropriate-size chunks, and boil in lightly salted water until just tender. Toss while still warm in the dressing, letting them marinate for as long as you wish.

Zucchini: scrub them, trim the two ends, but do not peel them. Boil whole in lightly salted water until barely tender. Cube them. Toss in dressing half an hour or so before serving.

Boston or Butter Lettuce Salad

Rosie very carefully separates each perfect leaf from the central stem, washes the leaves with care in a basin of water, drains them on a towel or in the dish drainer, then gently surrounds them with clean towels and a plastic bag, and refrigerates them. Half an hour or so before serving, she arranges them stem down and smallest leaves in the center in a big bowl, so that the salad looks like an enormous head of lettuce sitting there. She covers the bowl with plastic wrap and refrigerates it, and just before serving she dribbles a *vinaigrette* dressing (for choices, see page 110), all around and over the leaves. No tossing is necessary, and serving is easy since one picks up the leaves without disturbing the design—at least until near the end.

Apple Turnover

I am particularly fond of the free-form turnover, since one can make it any size and shape, from mini to gargantuan. Round is pretty, but either square or rectangular is more practical because it uses less dough and the leftovers are evenly shaped and therefore easily turned into decorations.

For 1 large turnover about 9 by 9 inches (23 x 23 cm), serving 6 to 8

Sweet pie dough
Pâte brisée fine, sucrée

1½ cups (215 g) all-purpose flour, unbleached preferred

½ cup (70 g) plain bleached cake flour

1½ sticks (6 ounces or 170 g) chilled unsalted butter and 2 Tb shortening

2 Tb sugar

¼ tsp salt

½ cup (1 dL), more or less, iced water

Other ingredients for the turnover

4 or 5 apples that will keep their shape in cooking, such as Golden Delicious, Rome Beauty, Newton, Monroe, Northern Spy

3 Tb or more sugar

½ tsp, more or less, powdered cinnamon (optional)

The grated rind and the juice of ½ lemon (optional)

1 Tb or more melted butter

Egg glaze (1 egg beaten in a cup with 1 tsp water)

Equipment

A food processor is dandy for making the dough; a rolling pin; a buttered pastry sheet; a pastry brush for glazing the tart

The dough

Of course you can make the dough by hand or in an electric mixer, but the food processor is sensationally fast and foolproof using these proportions. Proceed as follows: with metal blade in place, measure the flours into the bowl of the machine, cut the butter rapidly into pieces the size of your little-finger joint, and drop into the flour, along with the sugar, shortening, and salt. Using the on-off flick technique lasting ½ second, process 7 to 8 flicks, just to start breaking up the butter. Then, with water poised over opening of machine, turn it on and pour in all but 1 tablespoon of the iced water. Process in spurts, on and off, just until dough begins to mass together but is still rough with some unformed bits. Turn it out onto your work surface and mass together rapidly with the heel of one hand into a somewhat rough cake. (Dough should be pliable—neither dry and hard nor, on the other hand, sticky. Pat in sprinkles more of all-purpose flour if sticky; cut into pieces and sprinkle on droplets more water if dry and hard, then re-form into a cake.) Wrap in plastic and refrigerate for at least an hour, to congeal the butter in the dough so that it will roll easily, and to allow the flour particles to absorb the water so that it will handle nicely and bake properly.

🕐 May be made 2 or 3 days in advance and refrigerated—but if you have used unbleached flour it will gradually turn grayish; it can still be baked at that point if only mildly discolored since it will whiten in the oven. Or freeze the dough, which is the best plan when you want to have ready dough available; defrost at room temperature or overnight in the refrigerator—dough should be cold and firm for easy rolling.

The apples

Quarter, core, and peel the apples, then cut into thinnish lengthwise slices. Toss in a mixing bowl with sugar and optional cinnamon and lemon rind and juice. Cover with plastic wrap and let macerate for 20 minutes or longer, so that apples will exude their excess juices.

Forming the turnover

Always work rapidly from here on to prevent the dough from softening; if it becomes difficult to handle, refrigerate it at once for 20 minutes or so, then continue.) Roll the chilled dough into a rectangle 20 inches long and 10 inches wide (50 x 25 cm) and trim off the edges with a pastry wheel or a knife—refrigerate trimmings for decorations later. Lightly flour surface of dough, fold in half end to end, and center on the buttered pastry sheet. Place a piece of wax paper at edge of fold, and unfold top of dough onto paper. Paint a border of cold water around the 3 edges of the bottom piece and pile the apples onto it, leaving a ¾-inch (2-cm) border free at the 3 edges. Sprinkle on more sugar, and a tablespoon or so of melted butter. Flip top of dough over onto the apples, and press edges firmly together, to seal. Turn up the 3 edges all around, then press a design into them (to seal further) with the tines of a table fork and, if you wish, press a decorative edging all around those sides with the back of a knife.

🕐 If you have time, it is a good idea at this point to refrigerate the turnover (covered lightly with plastic wrap) for half an hour (or for several hours); it will bake more evenly when the dough has had time to relax, and you, in turn, will have time to turn your leftover bits of dough into a mock puff pastry which will rise into a splendid design.

Mock puff pastry decorations
(For massed scraps about the size of a half tennis ball)

Knead leftover raw pastry scraps briefly into a cake, roll into a rectangle, and spread 1 teaspoon of butter down two-thirds of its length. Fold into 3 as though folding a business letter; repeat with another roll-out, buttering, and fold-up. Wrap and refrigerate for 20 to 30 minutes, then roll and fold (but omit butter) 2 more times. For the simple decorations I used on this turnover, roll out again into a rectangle about 10 inches (25 cm) long, and cut into 5 strips about ¼ inch (¾ cm) wide. Refrigerate, covered, until ready to use.

Decorating and baking the turnover

Preheat oven to 400°F/200°C. Paint top of turnover lightly with cold water. To simulate wrapping ribbon for your turnover "parcel," crisscross 2 strips of dough, laying them from corner to corner; lay 1 crosswise from top to bottom, and a final one horizontally, as shown. Loop the final strip into a loose knot and place on top. Pierce 2 steam holes 1/16 inch (¼ cm) in diameter in top of dough with the point of a knife, going down through the dough to the apples. Paint top of dough and decorations with a coating of egg glaze, wait a moment, and paint on another coat. (Egg glaze goes on just the moment before baking.) Make crosshatchings in the glaze with the back of a knife or the tines of a table fork—to give it a more interesting texture when baked.

Set turnover in the middle level of preheated oven and bake for 20 minutes, then check to see if it is browning too much. It bakes 35 to 40 minutes in all, and does best at high heat so the pastry will crisp; if it seems to be cooking too fast, turn oven down a little and/or cover top of turnover loosely with foil. It is done when bottom has browned nicely and when juices begin to bubble out of steam holes. Remove from oven and slide it out onto a rack. Serve hot, warm, or cold. You may wish to accompany the turnover with vanilla ice cream, fresh cream, lightly whipped and sweetened cream, or custard sauce.

Remarks:

Other sizes, other fillings. You can, of course, make turnovers any size and shape you wish, and you can use all sorts of fillings as long as they are not too juicy. Always macerate fresh fruit first with sugar and lemon to force out their excess juices, and a very juicy fruit should first be cooked. Canned fruits or jams bake well in turnovers, as do all sorts of dried nut and fruit mixtures.

Pie and Quiche Dough:

Use the same proportions of butter, flour, and water for meat pies, turnovers, and quiches but omit the sugar and increase the salt to ¾ teaspoon in all.

⏱ *Timing*

Wait till you hear the doorbell ring before drizzling dressing on the lettuce salad. Your only other last-minute job is the pleasant one of arranging beautiful platters and setting them out. Part of the skewered salad and the dressing can be prepared that morning, but the skewering itself, and the brief marination of mushrooms, cherry tomatoes, zucchini, and peppers, is done half an hour before guests are due.

Otherwise, all your preparations can be made the day before; and the turnover dough can be frozen. While the Chicken Melon roasts, you can cook the hard-boiled eggs, make mayonnaise, and prepare some of the salad vegetables: artichokes, onions, potatoes, topinambours, and turnips.

If you've never boned a chicken before, it's wise to make your first attempt at a leisurely pace, giving yourself time to stop frequently and take a fix on your location in the sometimes bewildering mass of flesh and bone. Once you've done it and understood it, this job is a breeze ever after, and takes little more time than, for example, carving a cooked bird.

Menu Variations

The Chicken Melon: You can bone, stuff, tie, and roast almost any bird, or bake it in a pastry crust (see *Mastering II*), or poach it instead of roasting it and finish with an aspic glaze. Or simply pack the *pâté* stuffing into a terrine and bake it that way, or bake it skinless in a pastry case. But if you have a crust here, you will not want one for dessert!

The salads: If you omit the potato salad, a loaf or two of French bread will provide starch. For the lettuce salad, when perfect leaf lettuce is unavailable, substitute one of the mixed salads in this book. The makeup of the skewered vegetable salad will be determined by the season anyway.

The Apple Turnover: You could make little individual turnovers by the same recipe— but baking time will be only 20 to 30 minutes. Or use the same dough to make a tart or tartlets: bake the shell or shells, waterproof the inside with a melted jelly glaze, arrange the fruit (cooked or not, depending on type), and glaze again (see *Mastering I* for a basic method).

Leftovers

The Chicken Melon: You might plan to have a little extra of the stuffing mixture and save it for a special meal! Lightly formed into little cakes, dredged with flour, and sautéed, it is a charming luncheon or first-course dish, something between a *quenelle* or mousse and a chickenburger, and can be given extra savor by a creamy, full-flavored *béchamel* sauce (for which you'd save every drop of degreased roasting juice). You can freeze an uncooked *pâté* mixture or the raw chicken melon itself; but few *pâtés* take kindly to freezing after cooking. However, a cooked, finished "melon" will keep a week under refrigeration.

The salads: The potato salad will keep in the refrigerator for 3 or 4 days; but not if it has sat at room temperature for any length of time. That's because mayonnaise, like any egg mixture, is vulnerable to bacterial action. If you have marinated vegetables to spare, why not dice them, fold into a mayonnaise, and serve on lettuce next day as a *macédoine* salad?

The Apple Turnover: If you have extra dough, refrigerate it or freeze it (see recipe) and use again (see Menu Variations). Extra macerated fruit can always be cooked gently, then puréed and used as a sauce for custard or rice pudding. The cooked turnover itself will freeze and may be reheated in the oven.

HB Eggs

An unusual and successful way to boil and peel them

The perfect hard-boiled egg is one that is perfectly unblemished when peeled; its white is tender, its yolk is nicely centered and just set, and no dark line surrounds it. Excess heat toughens the egg, and excess heat also causes that dark line between yolk and white. To illustrate such a perfect estate, way back in the 1960s I did a whole television program on this earth-shaking subject, calling it "HB Eggs." No sooner was it aired than our French Chef office was flooded with suggestions, some of which were very useful indeed. As an example, one viewer suggested the use of an egg pricker, an instrument that pierces the shell at the large end to release the contents of its ever-present air pocket; if the air is allowed to remain it will expand when the egg heats, and that sometimes causes the shell to crack.

The most interesting idea came from the Georgia Egg Board, and the reason they got into the picture is that Georgia is a breeding ground not only for Presidents and peaches, but also for millions of eggs boiled and peeled by home cooks and especially by business enterprises. Because of the egg's commercial importance, scientists at the University of Georgia undertook a study involving over 800 of them and concluded that the best way of shrinking the egg body from the shell, to make for easy peeling, was to plunge the just-boiled eggs into iced water for one minute, meanwhile bringing the cooking water back to the boil, then to plunge the eggs into boiling water for ten seconds, and right after that to peel them. The iced water shrinks egg from shell, and the subsequent short boil expands shell from egg.

I tried out the Georgia method, found it good, and described it in my monthly column for *McCall's* magazine, thereby receiving even more new suggestions, including one from a testy 74-year-old asking if the U. of Georgia had nothing better to do! They should ask their grandmothers, said she who has been boiling eggs since she was a little girl: she boils them 12 to 15 minutes, plunges them into cold water, and has never had the slightest bit of trouble peeling them.

However, since an actual boil really does produce a tough egg, the Georgia people will just tolerate a simmer but prefer what I call "the 17-minute sit-in," where eggs are submerged in a pan of cold water, brought to the boil, then covered and removed from heat to remain for 17 minutes before their rapid cooling and peeling. I was therefore skeptical indeed when a letter came from the American Egg Board in Chicago outlining a series of experiments conducted by the Department of Poultry Science at the University of Wisconsin, using—of all things—the pressure cooker. How did they ever dream that up? I wonder. But it works very well indeed, and here is how to go about it.

HB eggs in the pressure cooker

1. Pour enough water into the pan of the cooker to cover the number of eggs you plan to cook—2 inches (5 cm) for 12 eggs is usually sufficient. Bring the water to the boil.

2. Meanwhile, wash the eggs in warm water with detergent to remove possible preserving spray from shells and to take the chill off the eggs. Rinse thoroughly. (Do not pierce them.)

3. Remove the pressure pan from heat, gently lower eggs into water, cover the pan, and bring rapidly to full (15 pounds) pressure. Immediately remove pan from heat and let sit under pressure for exactly five minutes.

4. At once release pressure, drain eggs, and cool them in cold water—or iced water.

5. Peel the eggs as soon as possible. I must admit that my first trial with this method gave me some qualms, but it worked— the eggs peeled beautifully. I kept at it, finding sometimes that the yolks were not entirely set at the very central point, but I never have had any trouble peeling. My last experiment was, I feel, pretty conclusive since I had managed to get some absolutely fresh eggs, laid by the young hens of a retired vicar on Cape Cod, each egg carefully dated on the large end. They were laid on a Sunday, boiled on a Monday,

and that's about as fresh a dozen eggs as I am ever likely to get. Here are the results:

1. Four eggs cooked by the coddle method (brought to the boil, removed from heat, covered, and let sit for 17 minutes). Two of these simply chilled in cold water—peeled with difficulty. Two of these chilled in iced water for 1 minute, plunged into boiling water for ten seconds, then chilled briefly and peeled —peeled with some difficulty but more easily than the first batch.

2. Four eggs done in the electric egg steamer/poacher. Peeled easily, but seemed a little tough. (And, by the way, mine poaches me a tough egg, too.)

3. Four eggs done in the pressure cooker. Peeled easily, and whites were tender.

Conclusion: The pressure cooker is great for HB eggs!

Peeling addendum

Two of my *McCall's* readers suggested a helpful peeling trick: after cracking the shells all over and peeling a circle of shell off the large end, slip an ordinary teaspoon between shell and egg and work it down the egg all around to the small end, manipulating the egg under a thin stream of cold water or in a bowl of water as you go.

The ugly dark line around the yolk on the left is due to excessive heat—the perfect HB egg is on the right.

An exquisite and fanciful luncheon menu for your most sophisticated acquaintances, under the Sign of the Smiling Fish.

VIP Lunch

Menu

*Apéritif: Kir au Champagne—Champagne
with black currant or raspberry liqueur*

❧

*Choulibiac—Fillets of sole and mushrooms
baked in choux pastry*

❧

*Watercress Salad with Endive and Cucumbers
Melba Toast or Toasted Pita Bread Triangles*

❧

Sorbet aux Poires—Fresh pear sherbet

❧

*Suggested wines:
A fine white Burgundy or Pinot Chardonnay*

This luncheon menu is elegant but not fussy, unusual but not eccentric, and eminently suitable for those occasions when you want to offer a charming surprise either to distinguished guests, or to friends well versed in cookery who enjoy innovative food and good wine. The main course, the Choulibiac, is so spectacular a dish in both its composition and its presentation that it needs nothing accompanying it. I follow it with a bit of greenery, and then end the meal with fresh pear sherbet —a delight of the purest and most refreshing kind. Therefore I serve no first course, and offer only a glass of chilled Champagne before the meal. To give a stylish and colorful touch, Paul adds a few drops of black currant or raspberry liqueur to each glass.

Such a creation as the Choulibiac was unthinkable in all but the grandest houses and greatest restaurants until a few years ago, when the invention of the food processor brought such culinary fantasies right to the ordinary kitchen's doorstep. Almost anyone now may produce with ease many a classical preparation of the *haute cuisine* (such as a velvety, airy mousse of fish, which once took hours of labor with mortar and pestle, then beating over constantly renewed bowls of ice, then forcing the mixture through hair-fine sieves). In addition, the basic elements are easily available. So the modern cook's imagination is freed to devise original and fanciful assemblages like the Choulibiac.

In its rococo style, it is almost a playful dish. Even its name is a pun on the Russian *coulibiac,* an envelope of brioche pastry stuffed with salmon, mushrooms, and *kasha*…and a very good dish, too, though a heavy one in comparison to this. The Choulibiac is so much lighter because it rests on a giant crêpe rather than on a layer of brioche dough, and it is encased in the thinnest possible cloak of *choux* or cream puff pastry—just enough to protect its overall inside covering of fish mousse, under which rest layers of the freshest of sole fillets interspersed with wine-flavored minced mushrooms.

What you present to your guests as the finished dish is a plump golden-brown pillow topped with a fat flirtatious fish, wearing such a broad smile that one knows he is proud to have become a Choulibiac. When sliced it is dark brown, white, and daffodil yellow—the

layering of mushroom *duxelles*, fish fillets, and fish mousse. Each serving is surrounded with a beautifully buttery yellow sauce.

After the salad, the silver-white pear sherbet seems to capture with icy intensity the flavor and perfume of a ripe pear at its fleeting peak. You can't always count on having perfect pears ready for a given day, and, if you do find some, you can't keep them. But this simple, artful recipe does seem to preserve their indescribable taste intact. You may discreetly enhance it with a touch of Williams pear brandy, which is sold by a few knowing shops to connoisseurs. (It comes with a plump pear lolling about in the bottle. When the pear tree buds, the bottle is slipped over a choice twig and acts as a little private greenhouse for the fruit which ripens inside it, and which will flavor the spirit.)

It seems a bit pedestrian, perhaps, for me to remind you that most of the elements of this meal—except for the final assemblage and baking—can be prepared long in advance, that it requires no novel or difficult techniques, and that it is not particularly expensive. Like so many delightful examples of the rococo, it is simply a happy combination of tried-and-true basic components; and, like them, it is sound and practical. It just happens to be great fun, too.

Preparations

Choulibiac is not a recipe I would attempt at all without a food processor. One could do it, of course, spending several hours mincing acres of mushrooms, grinding the fish, beating over ice—but not me! I'd pick another recipe, and I have made suggestions for variations and alternatives in Menu Variations later in the chapter. And you do need an ice-cream maker with dasher for the sherbet.

Marketing and Storage:
Staples to have on hand

Salt
White and black peppercorns ▼
Nutmeg
Mustard, the strong Dijon type
Olive oil and cooking oil
Optional: semisweet chocolate (4 ounces or 115 g); unsweetened chocolate (1 ounce or 30 g)
Sugar (instant superfine useful but not essential)
Instant-blending flour (⅓ cup or ¾ dL), useful but not essential ▼
All-purpose flour
Milk
Heavy cream (1 to 2 cups or ¼ to ½ L)
Butter (½ to 1 pound or 225 to 450 g, depending on the way you make the sauce for the Choulibiac)
Eggs (8 "large")
Lemons (4)
Shallots and/or scallions
Onion, carrot, celery stalk, and imported bay leaf—for fish stock
Wines and liqueurs: dry white French vermouth and Cognac

Specific ingredients for this menu

Coarse salt (2 pounds or 1 kg) for freezing sherbet
Sole fillets (about 2 pounds or 900 g, 16 skinless and boneless pieces about 9 by 2 inches or 23 x 5 cm)
Halibut fillets or additional sole (½ pound or 225 g)
Fresh fish trimmings (enough to make about 2 cups or ½ L), for fish stock ▼
Fresh mushrooms (1 quart or 10 ounces or 285 g)
Cucumbers (2)
Watercress (2 or 3 bunches)
Belgian endive (3 or 4 heads)
Fresh parsley (1 bunch)
Optional: fresh dill weed (a stalk or two)
Optional: cherry tomatoes (about 1½ dozen), for salad
Melba toast or toasted pita bread triangles
Pears (5 or 6 ripe, full-of-flavor)
Pear liqueur (Eau-de-Vie de Poire Williams recommended)
Champagne (1 bottle)
Crème de cassis or liqueur de framboise (¼ bottle black currant or raspberry liqueur)
Dry Port or Sercial Madeira

▶ *Remarks:*

Staples

White peppercorns: not always to be found on supermarket shelves, these can be had bottled at specialty shops. White pepper, used in most fish dishes or white sauces, is the mature pepper berry with its husk rubbed off; black is the dried immature berry. *Instant-blending flour:* the patented granular type, which is so useful for crêpes; if you can't find it, use regular flour in the recipe, as indicated.

Ingredients for this menu

Fish stock: to make the sauce for the Choulibiac; or use a hollandaise sauce, as described on page 11 (but you will probably want to omit the *béchamel* stabilizer needed for that Breakfast Party holding operation). *Pears:* most pears as you buy them are not fully ripe, but some, if they were picked when immature, will never ripen. Therefore, look for firm flesh that has just begun to soften. The best pears for your sherbet are full-flavored varieties like Bartlett (buy when turning yellowish or rosy), or Anjou or Comice (buy yellow-green). Be careful there is no weakening of the flesh near the stem (an indication the pear is immature); avoid wilting or shriveling flesh, dull skin with no gloss, and spots on the sides or at the blossom (large) end of the fruit. Ripen for a few days at room temperature in a closed paper bag or a ripening device (the purpose of either is to trap the harmless—indeed benign— ethylene gas exuded by ripening fruit). A nearly ripe apple or tomato, enclosed with your pears, will hasten the work. When perfectly ripe, the skin color is yellower or rosier and the pear is very fragrant. At this point, chill if you can't use at once; but don't wait long.

Choulibiac

Fillets of sole baked with mushrooms and fish mousse in a choux pastry crust

This free-form rectangular structure built upon a giant crêpe is an elegant creation and definitely *grande cuisine*, but parts of it may be assembled bit by bit, as you have time—and as you will see from the following recipe.

For a rectangular Choulibiac about 12 by 5 by 2½ inches (30 x 13 x 6½ cm), serving 6 to 8 people

Batter for Giant Crêpe
Baked in an 11-by-17-inch (27-x-42-cm) jelly roll pan, nonstick if possible

⅓ cup (¾ dL) Wondra or instant-blending flour, or all-purpose flour
½ cup (1 dL) milk
1 "large" egg
1 Tb cooking oil
½ tsp salt

Pâte à choux
About 3 cups (¾ L), for fish mousse and for encasing Choulibiac

1½ cups (3½ dL) water in a heavy-bottomed 2½-quart (2½-L) saucepan
6 ounces (1½ sticks or 180 g) butter, cut into ½-inch (1½-cm) pieces
1½ tsp salt
1 cup (¼ L) flour (measure by scooping dry-measure cup into flour and sweeping off excess)
6 "large" eggs

Filling ingredients

16 skinless and boneless sole fillets (each about 9 x 2 inches, or 23 x 5 cm), or about 2 pounds (900 g)

½ pound (225 g) skinless and boneless halibut, or more sole fillets

1 cup (¼ L) heavy cream, chilled

1 quart (10 ounces or 285 g) fresh mushrooms

Miscellaneous

Several shallots and/or scallions

A little Cognac and 3 Tb dry Port or Sercial Madeira

Salt, freshly ground white pepper, ground nutmeg

4 or more Tb butter (for greasing pans, sautéing, etc.)

4 funnels made of aluminum foil (twisted around a pencil), ⅓ inch (¾ cm) in diameter and 1 inch (2½ cm) long

Egg glaze (1 egg beaten with 1 tsp water in a small bowl)

3 cups (¾ L) white-wine sauce (next recipe) or hollandaise, page 11, to serve with the Choulibiac

Equipment

You need a sturdy, level jelly-roll pan, preferably with a nonstick surface. An old battered pan is going to produce an uneven crêpe since the batter is spread so thin—there may even be areas that are not covered, while other areas, where the batter settles, will be too thick. Also, your oven must be absolutely level. If you don't have reliable equipment, make two large, thin crêpes in your biggest frying pan, then piece them together to obtain approximately the dimensions called for in the final assembling.

The giant crêpe

Place the flour in a mixing bowl and beat in the milk, egg, oil, and salt; let rest for 10 minutes. Meanwhile preheat oven to 400°F/200°C, smear jelly-roll pan with a tablespoon of soft butter, roll flour in it, and knock out excess. Pour crêpe batter into pan to a depth of about ⅛ inch (½ cm), and set in lower level of oven for 4 to 5 minutes, until batter has set. Then place pan 4 to 5 inches (10 to 13 cm) under a medium-hot broiler element to brown top of crêpe slowly and lightly—it will seethe and bubble a bit as it browns but do not let it overcook and stiffen. Remove from oven and with a flexible-blade spatula carefully loosen crêpe all around from edges to center of pan. If it sticks, it has not cooked quite long enough; return to lower level of oven 2 to 3 minutes more. Slide crêpe off onto a cake rack.

❷ You may roll crêpe, when cool, between two sheets of wax paper and refrigerate, or wrap airtight and freeze.

Seasoning the fish fillets

Mince enough shallots or scallions to make 3 tablespoons and set aside in a small bowl, reserving half for the mushrooms later. Choose a rectangular or oval dish 10 to 12 inches (25 to 30 cm) long, sprinkle 1 teaspoon shallots on the bottom, and arrange over them a layer of overlapping sole fillets; season lightly with salt and pepper, a sprinkling of minced shallots or scallions, a few drops of Cognac, and continue with the rest of the fillets, making probably three layers in all. Cover with plastic wrap and refrigerate. (Set over ice if wait is more than a few hours.)

The pâte à choux
Bring the 1½ cups (3½ dL) water rather slowly to the boil with the cut-up butter and the salt. As soon as butter has melted, remove from heat and immediately dump in all of the cup (¼ L) of flour at once, beating vigorously with a portable mixer and/or wooden spoon. When smooth, set over moderately high heat and beat for several minutes until mixture begins to film the bottom of the pan—indicating excess moisture has boiled off.

When using a food processor, scrape hot paste into machine, activate it, and break in 5 eggs rapidly, one after the other, then stop the machine. (Do the same if you have a table model mixer, beating just until each egg is absorbed before adding the next. By hand,

make a well in center of hot paste in saucepan, then beat in 5 eggs one by one with either a portable mixer or a wooden spoon. Break sixth egg into a bowl, blend yolk and white with a fork, and how much to add to the paste depends on its thickness—it should just hold its shape in a spoon. Beat in as much of the final egg by droplets as you judge safe, remembering the more egg the more the pastry puffs, but you don't want the batter to thin out too much.)

Remove ½ cup (1 dL) of the *choux* pastry to a medium-size metal mixing bowl and reserve for fish mousse, next step. For the food processor, scrape paste back into the saucepan, and do not wash out processor; simply replace blade; cover pastry with plastic wrap, set in a pan of warm but not too hot water, and hold for final assembly.

The fish mousse
Set the reserved bowl of *choux* pastry in a larger bowl with a tray of ice cubes and water to cover them, and stir several minutes with a wooden spoon to chill; leave over ice. For the food processor, cut the halibut and one of the sole fillets into ½-inch (1½-cm) pieces and place in the processor with the cold *choux* paste, ¾ cup (1¾ dL) chilled cream, ½ teaspoon salt, several grinds white pepper, and a big pinch nutmeg; activate the processor for about a minute, until the fish is ground into a fine paste. If still stiff, beat in more cream by dribbles—mousse must be just firm enough to hold its shape for spreading; scrape out of food processor into *choux*-paste bowl; do not wash processor; simply replace blade and use for mushrooms, next step. (Lacking a processor, put fish twice through finest blade of meat grinder and beat resulting purée into the *choux* paste over ice; then, with a portable mixer, beat in the seasonings and, by driblets, as much of the cream as the mixture will take and still hold its shape.)

Cover bowl with plastic wrap and, still over ice, refrigerate.

● Or cover airtight and freeze if wait is longer than 12 hours.

The mushroom duxelles

Trim the mushrooms, wash rapidly, and if you are using a food processor, chop by hand into ½-inch (1½-cm) pieces, then mince 1 cup (¼ L) at a time in the processor—flipping it on and off every second just until mushrooms are cut into ⅛-inch (½-cm) pieces; otherwise mince by hand with a big knife. To extract juices, either squeeze in a potato ricer or twist by handfuls in the corner of a towel. Sauté in a frying pan, in 2 tablespoons hot butter and 1 tablespoon minced shallots or scallions until mushroom pieces begin to separate from each other—4 to 5 minutes over moderately high heat, stirring. Season lightly with salt and pepper, pour in 3 tablespoons Port or Madeira, and boil down rapidly to evaporate liquid. Scrape the *duxelles* into a bowl and reserve.

● If done in advance, cool, cover, and either refrigerate for up to 4 or 5 days, or freeze.

Assembling the Choulibiac

Spread the giant crêpe, browned side down, on a buttered baking sheet (nonstick if possible) and trim off any stiff edges with scissors. Spread ⅓ of the fish mousse in a rectangle about 12 inches (30 cm) long and 5 inches (13 cm) wide down the center, and over it arrange ½ of the fish fillets, slightly overlapping. On top of that spread ½ of the mushroom *duxelles*, then the rest of the fish fillets and remaining *duxelles*. Beat any fish-seasoning juices into reserved mousse, spread mousse over top and sides of fish structure, then bring the ends and sides of the crêpe (cutting out the corners) up over the fish. Trim off excess crêpe, leaving a side edging on top of only 1 inch (2½ cm). Reserve ½ cup (1 dL) or so of pastry for final decorations; then, using a flexible-blade spatula dipped in cold water, spread ⅛ inch (½ cm) *choux* pastry evenly over top and sides, masking the structure completely. Poke holes ⅛ inch (½ cm) across and ½ inch (1½ cm) deep, angled toward center of structure, in the lower part of each of the four corners, and insert buttered foil funnels (to drain out any juices during baking).

● Refrigerate the Choulibiac if you are not continuing—but plan to bake it within a few hours.

Final decorations and baking

Baking time: about 45 minutes
Preheat oven to 425°F/220°C and set rack in lower middle level. If *choux* pastry has cooled and stiffened, beat over hot water to soften and warm to tepid only; spoon it into a pastry bag with ½-inch (1½-cm) cannelated tube. Paint Choulibiac with a coating of egg glaze, then pipe *choux* pastry decorations onto it— such as the fanciful outline of a fish with mouth, eyes, fins; or a zigzag border all around the edges and a number of rosettes on top. Glaze the decorations, and the rest of the pastry, with two coatings of egg.

Immediately set in oven and bake for 15 to 20 minutes at 425°F/220°C, or until the pastry top has begun to brown and to puff slightly; turn thermostat down to 375°F/190°C and continue baking another 20 min-

utes or so. Choulibiac is done when you begin to smell a delicious odor of pastry, fish, and mushrooms, and, finally, when juices start to exude onto baking sheet. (Pastry will not puff a great deal, just slightly.)

Plan to serve as soon as possible, although the Choulibiac will stay warm in turned-off oven, door ajar, for 20 to 30 minutes—the longer it sits the more of its vital fish juices will exude. Loosen bottom of Choulibiac carefully from pastry sheet, using a flexible-blade spatula, and slide it onto a hot platter or a serving board.

To serve, cut into crosswise pieces from one of the short sides and surround each portion with sauce—either the following, which can be made well ahead, or hollandaise (see page 11).

Sauce Vin Blanc:

White wine velouté sauce

For about 2½ cups

If you plan on this sauce for the Choulibiac, save out 5 to 6 tablespoons of the *choux* pastry (scrapings from the pastry bag, for instance), and the sauce is practically made, except for the white-wine fish stock. Here's how to go about it, in a rather free-form way.

2 cups (½ L) fresh fish trimmings (or extra sole or halibut)
1 small onion, chopped
½ carrot, chopped
1 small celery stalk, sliced
8 to 10 parsley stems (not leaves)
1 imported bay leaf
1 cup (¼ L) dry white French vermouth
1 cup (¼ L) water
½ tsp salt (and more as needed)
5 to 6 Tb ready-made *choux* pastry in a bowl
About 1 cup (¼ L) milk
About ½ cup (1 dL) heavy cream
White pepper
Drops of fresh lemon juice
Softened unsalted butter, as your conscience permits

Simmer the fish trimmings or fish with the vegetables, herbs, wine, water, and ½ teaspoon salt for 20 to 30 minutes; strain, then boil down rapidly to 1 cup. Gradually blend into the *choux* pastry, pour into saucepan, and simmer, thinning out as necessary with spoonfuls of milk and cream. Sauce should coat a spoon lightly; season carefully with additional salt, pepper, and drops of lemon juice.

🕐 If made in advance, clean sauce off sides of pan and float a spoonful of cream over surface to prevent a skin from forming. Bring to the simmer before proceeding.

Just before serving, taste again carefully for seasoning, then remove from heat and beat in softened butter by spoonfuls. (Just a spoonful or two will enrich the sauce nicely, but you may beat in as many more, almost, as you wish, as though you were making a hollandaise.)

Watercress Salad with Endive and Cucumbers

The salad should really be served after the Choulibiac, but this depends on your table and service arrangements. Whether to serve it on a platter or in a big bowl, or arrange each serving individually—which can be very attractive —is also a matter of your choice and facilities. Pass the Melba toast or pita separately.

For 6 people

2 or 3 bunches watercress, depending on size

2 cucumbers

3 or 4 heads Belgian endive

1 tsp Dijon-type prepared mustard

1 Tb fresh lemon juice

4 to 5 Tb best-quality light olive oil or salad oil

Salt and pepper

Fresh minced dill weed or parsley, halved cherry tomatoes (optional)

Trim off tough stems from watercress, wash the cress, spin dry, and wrap loosely in a clean towel; refrigerate in a plastic bag. Peel the cucumbers, slice thin, and refrigerate in a bowl of salted water; drain thoroughly and dry in a towel before serving. Separate the leaves from the central stems of the endive and refrigerate in a damp towel and plastic bag. Place the mustard, lemon juice, and oil in a screw-topped jar, season with salt and pepper, shake to blend, taste, and correct seasoning.

At serving time, toss each ingredient separately in a little of the dressing (well shaken first), correct seasoning for each, and make your arrangement. One I like is to place the endives first, like the spokes of a wheel, then make a bed of cress, and a topping of cucumber slices. (You may also like a sprinkling of fresh minced dill or parsley tossed with your cucumbers, and a few halved cherry tomatoes placed around for color.)

Fresh Pear Sherbet

For about 1 quart

5 or 6 fine ripe pears, to make about 2 cups (½ L) purée

2 lemons

¾ cup (1 ¾ dL) sugar—instant superfine, if possible (for fast dissolving)

1 egg white

3 to 4 Tb best-quality white pear liqueur, such as Eau-de-Vie de Poire Williams (optional but highly recommended)

Equipment

A dasher-type ice-cream freezer; crushed ice; coarse salt; a vegetable mill or food processor for puréeing pears

Note: I have tried this sherbet in machines other than the old-fashioned dasher type, and have not been pleased with the results, which are not as smooth. The non-dasher ice-tray method is unsatisfactory, since the sherbet needs beating. I am sure the one-unit freezer-dasher luxury-priced electric machine would do a beautiful job.

Wash the pears and lemons. Grate the rind of 1 lemon into a large mixing bowl, and strain the juice of both (or 4 tablespoons) into the bowl. Quarter, peel, and core the pears, and cut into chunks; toss, as you do them, in the bowl with the lemon and a sprinkling of the sugar. (Lemon and sugar prevent the pears from darkening, and you want to keep them white.) Immediately the pears are prepared, purée them with the lemon juice, adding the rest of the sugar and puréeing until you are sure all sugar granules have dissolved completely. (Test by tasting.) If you used a food processor for puréeing, add the egg white to the container and purée a moment more. Otherwise, beat the egg white in a small bowl until it forms soft peaks and fold into the pear purée.

Prepare ice-cream freezer, using 1 part coarse salt to every 4 parts crushed ice. (The salt lowers the temperature of the ice. And it is important that the ice be finely crushed: if you use cubed or coarsely chipped ice, the salt slips down to the bottom and will have no freezing effect.) Pour pear purée into freezing container; if you are using it, stir in the pear liqueur only at the last moment, so that it hasn't time to darken the pears. Freeze the

sherbet, which will take about 25 minutes; then pack it in a sealed airtight container and store in the freezer for at least 4 hours to cure. (Sherbet does not develop its full flavor until it has cured.) Set in refrigerator for 20 to 30 minutes before serving to let it soften.

🕐   Sherbet may be made several days in advance, although it gradually loses its freshly made texture and develops crystals that make it less smooth—in that case you could let it soften, and freeze again in the ice-cream machine.

A pretty way to serve this sherbet is to spoon it into goblets and stick a chocolate heart in each helping.

To Make Chocolate Hearts:

Melt 4 ounces (115 g) semisweet and 1 ounce (30 g) unsweetened chocolate: break it up into a small saucepan, cover and set in a larger pan of boiling water, remove from heat and let sit 5 minutes or so, until soft; then stir up to make a smooth shining mass. Remove pan from heat and stir with a wooden spoon until bottom of pan is almost cold to your hand. Then spread an even 3/16-inch (¾-cm) layer on wax paper over a baking sheet and let cool until it clouds over and is almost set. Press heart designs into chocolate with a small cookie cutter (or outline hearts in the chocolate with the point of a small knife), and peel paper and surrounding chocolate from each heart. Store on wax paper in refrigerator or freezer, and handle with wooden or rubber-covered tongs.

🕐 *Timing*

Despite its elegant character, this is not a tricky meal. Just remember to put the sherbet in the refrigerator to soften before you sit down to lunch or before the salad course, depending on whether your guests are lingerers or gobblers. The Choulibiac will stay warm for almost half an hour in the turned-off oven, though it does exude juice. (Incidentally, if it does, add the juices to your sauce.) Ideally, you'd start baking it when you fix the salad, about 15 minutes before your guests come. You can assemble it first thing in the morning and refrigerate it until time to bake. Also during the morning, make its sauce, chill your wine, and prepare your salad ingredients.

You can make the sherbet several days beforehand; you can make and freeze the crêpe, the fish mousse, the *duxelles,* and the chocolate hearts any time; and the *choux* pastry will keep 2 or 3 days in the refrigerator —but remember to reheat it just to tepid, beating it over hot water, so that it will be soft enough for easy spreading.

Menu Variations

Choulibiac: You can omit the *choux*-paste envelope and the giant pancake, and simply pile and bake fish fillets, layered with fish mousse, on a bed of *duxelles.* The dish is done when the fillets begin to shrink and exude juice (which you drain off—it's easy with a bulb baster; you rapidly reduce the juices and add them to your sauce). Or you can roll the fillets around the mousse, poach them in wine and fish stock on the bed of *duxelles,* reduce this liquid, and turn it into a sauce. *Mastering I* and

J.C.'s Kitchen both contain classic dishes of fillets of sole with mushrooms; there are fish and mushroom soufflés; and the combination is excellent in a *vol-au-vent* case. Or—but this is really an alternative, not a variation—you could return to the Choulibiac's Russian ancestor and make a *coulibiac;* there is a home-style version of that in *The French Chef Cookbook.*

Pear sherbet: If you can't obtain first-rate pears at their peak of flavor, pick another fruit for this recipe, like fresh peaches or pine-apple, or canned apricots. Or try the non-cranking sherbet recipes in *Mastering II* and *J.C.'s Kitchen.*

Leftovers

You can keep opened *Champagne* in its origi-nal bottle. Just look around for a patent metal Champagne cork that clamps on the top of the bottle and keeps in the fizz; store the bottle in the refrigerator.

The Choulibiac can be reheated in foil, but be sure to serve it with sauce, either the Vin Blanc or a hollandaise. You could serve left-overs as a cold first course or as another lunch-eon dish if you scrape off the *choux*-paste covering and the crêpe bottom; mask the fish attractively with a sour cream sauce or home-made mayonnaise lightened with sour cream or minced cucumbers. Or you could chop or purée the remains and stir them into a cream of

fish soup, a cream of celery soup, or a leek and potato soup, adding more cream or sour cream as need be.

Fish sauce can be frozen and mixed into a new sauce, or stirred into a fish soup as a special enrichment.

Leftover salad is leftover salad, to my mind, and has little charm for me except possi-bly at breakfast the next day, or washed off immediately and chopped up for addition to a vegetable soup of the minestrone type.

The sherbet can be refrozen. See notes about this at the end of the recipe.

Postscript: On playing with your food

Some children like to make castles out of their rice pudding, or faces with raisins for eyes. It is forbidden—so sternly that, when they grow up, they take a horrid revenge by dyeing me-ringues pale blue or baking birthday cakes in the form of horseshoes or lyres or whatnot. That is not playing with food, that is trifling.

"Play" to me means freedom and delight, as in the phrase "play of imagination." If cooks did not enjoy speculating about new possibilities in every method and each raw material, their art would stagnate and they would become rote performers, not creators. True cooks love to set one flavor against another in the imagination, to experiment with the great wealth of fresh produce in the super-markets, to bake what previously they braised, to try new devices. We all have flops, of course, but we learn from them; and, when an inven-tion or a variation works out at last, it is an enormous pleasure to propose it to our fellows.

Let's all play with our food, I say, and, in so doing, let us advance the state of the art together.

A splendid lunch for VIPs or favorite guests.

Lobster Soufflé for Lunch

Menu
For 6 people

Lobster Soufflé —on a Platter
Salade Mimosa
Pumpernickel Melba

❧

Les Délices aux Poires —A pear dessert

❧

Suggested wines:
A fine white Burgundy, Graves, or
chardonnay with the lobster, and a sweet
white wine or Champagne with the pears

Even in the days when lobsters were common as pea gravel, they were prized like rubies by great chefs, who joyfully elaborated on their intense flavor and azalea coloring to create sophisticated dishes for the most elegant occasions. And family cooks loved to call out, "Have another, anybody?" over big red clattering piles of lobsters simply boiled in the shell. Recent experiments in commercial lobster farming give us hope that those days will return, but for the moment lobsters are mighty scarce. In natural conditions, only one in one thousand infant lobsters will survive the predators of its critical first three weeks, during which time it lives near the sea's surface and is frequently in molt; thereafter it takes six years (in northern waters) to attain a weight of one pound. So it will be a while before we can make up for a century of overfishing. Consequently, we think twice nowadays about serving lobster: *whether* to as well as *how* to. Luckily—as happens so often in cookery—the second question can be turned around karate-wise to resolve the first.

While it's expensive indeed to offer guests a lobster apiece, let alone seconds, you *can* offer a richly lobstery dish, affordably, elegantly, and without waste—though "stretching a lobster" sounds like the oddest, if not neatest, trick of the week. These crustaceans have more ——s (I'm in need of a word like "ergs" or "amps" here, for units of flavor) per milligram than almost any other foodstuff: the —— s are lodged in the shells themselves and in every cranny thereof. So take advantage of those shells, by chopping, then sautéing them until they yield their all to a lovely sauce (well, not quite all; after that the shells can still go into the stockpot and produce a fine lobster broth—that's how flavorful they are). Use every morsel but the small stomach sac (which enfolds the tiny, crowned, blue-robed "lady"); amplify the flavor with butter, aromatics, wine, spirits, and flame; enhance the rich texture with crisp croutons and a savory soufflé blanket, and you will find that the meat of two or three small lobsters, or one middle-sized, easily serves six.

The model for this idea is a classic dish, which was not devised in the first place for reasons of economy. It originated at the Plaza-Athénée Hotel in Paris, which in the old days was reputed to have the most exquisite cuisine-for-the-happy-few imaginable. Its base is the famous lobster *à l'américaine,* whose name is a pedant's delight. Chauvinists among French gastronomes say that nothing so delicious could possibly be American; the word, they claim, is a corruption of *armoricaine,* derived from *Armorique,* the romantic old name for Brittany, whose cold seas certainly do produce good lobster. Not so, retort the anti-*armoricaines,* the dish contains tomatoes and Brittany is not tomato country. It was surely invented in Paris, they affirm, probably by a tomato-loving chef with a Mediterranean background, and it was named for an American client, or for the Americas from which tomatoes came. The argument will continue, and we shall never know the truth. But back to those lobsters.

Mounding a soufflé over the lobster meat was the Plaza-Athénée's contribution to elegance. But why not bake it on a platter, rather than in a soufflé dish? It makes for a splendidly dramatic presentation, for easy serving, and for a rather sturdier party offering. While the soufflé doesn't rise as high as if baked in a dish, it doesn't have as far to fall. Though it takes a bit of doing, you can prepare most of it the day before. And, once you add this wonderful concoction to your repertoire, you have added the possibility of a grand array of easy variants.

The flavor is robust as well as subtle, and, especially at lunch, I like something simple and delicate to follow. Salade Mimosa, gold and pale green, soothes the excited palate; Melba toast makes an even crisper contrast if you do it with pumpernickel. A poached pear has a lovely cool suavity; you can dress it up and enhance its fragrance with a chocolate base—perhaps tucking in a wine-soaked macaroon as a buffer—and add a satiny caramel sauce at the last moment. Its smoothness, the pear's velvet grain, and the friable chocolate combine incomparably.

Chocolate cups may strike you as old hat, and, moreover, tricky to make. Well, I haven't seen one since the thirties. Is that old hat or is that classic? And in working out the recipe through many trials and experiments, our cooking team found that the cups are quite easy to form if you use chocolate bits, with their slight extra viscosity, and then chill them well before peeling off the paper cases that serve as molds. With its pretty serrated edge and finely fluted sides, the chocolate case looks as airy as a dry autumn leaf. But it's not riskily fragile. The pear squats on it with all the confidence of Queen Victoria, who never looked around for a chair but just lowered away, calmly relying on the alertness of her equerries. This royal reference is no accident, for here is a lunch befitting any palace.

Open the sand sack in the lobster's head—there is the "lady" enshrined. Her blue robe turns red when cooked.

Preparations and Marketing

Recommended Equipment:

To cook the lobsters, a casserole or kettle; to get at the meat, lobster shears, page 60, are useful; to bake and serve the soufflé, a large ovenproof platter, oval preferred, or a shallow baking dish.

Paper baking cups (cupcake size) are ideal molds for the chocolate cases; for added stability, they may be set in flat-bottomed custard cups, shells, small bowls, or large muffin tins. We flattened out our paper cups a trifle, to accommodate our fine big pears.

Macaroons are heavy work without a food processor.

Staples to Have on Hand:

Salt
White and black peppercorns
Hot pepper sauce
Dried tarragon
Optional: dried oregano, thyme, or herb mixture
Garlic
Cream of tartar
Stick cinnamon or powdered cinnamon
Prepared mustard
Pure almond extract
Tomato paste or tomato sauce
Olive oil or fresh peanut oil
Flour
Unsalted butter
Milk

Specific Ingredients for This Menu:

Lobster, boiled or steamed: one 2 to 2½ pounds (1 to 1¼ kg) or two or three 1-pounders (450 g) ▼
Lobster stock, fish stock, or chicken broth (1 cup or ¼ L)
Beef stock or bouillon (½ cup or 1 dL)

Swiss cheese (a 6-ounce or 180-g piece)

Parmesan or mixed hard cheeses (see pumpernickel Melba recipe; 2 ounces or 60 g)

Pumpernickel or rye bread, unsliced

Nonsweet homemade-type white bread

Eggs (9 or 10 "large")

Heavy cream (1 cup or ¼ L)

Chocolate bits or morsels (12 ounces or 340 g, or 2 cups or ½ L)

Almond paste (see macaroon recipe; 8 ounces or 225 g)

Sugar (3½ cups or 8 dL; 700 g)

Fresh green herbs: such as parsley, basil, chives, tarragon

Lettuce: Boston, butter, or romaine (1 or 2 heads, depending on size)

Good-sized ripe unblemished pears: Anjou, Comice, or Bartlett (6)

Ripe red tomatoes (6 to 8 medium)

Carrots (1 medium)

Onions (1 medium)

Lemons (1)

Dry white wine or dry white French vermouth (4 cups or 1 L)

Optional: rum or bourbon whiskey

Cognac (⅓ cup or ¾ dL)

▶   **Remarks:**

Lobster: many fish markets carry ready-cooked lobsters. To boil or steam your own, which is usually more satisfactory, see recipe. Hen (female) lobsters are more desirable, since they contain coral (roe), to give your sauce extra red color. In buying live lobsters, choose the most active specimens; in buying ready-cooked ones, be sure that the tail is tightly curled and snaps back when pulled straight. Live lobsters can be kept for a day or 2 in the refrigerator, in paper bags pierced with a pencil for air.

Lobster Soufflé— on a Platter

A Plaza-Athénée-like soufflé accompanied by the famous lobster sauce à l'américaine

Manufacturing Note:

Although the classic recipe for lobster *à l'américaine* calls for it being cut up raw, sautéed, then simmered in its sauce, I have found that boiled lobster meat is a perfectly satisfactory alternative in this recipe, where the meat is seasoned with sauce made from the shells before the soufflé is mounded upon it. Boil the lobster, pick out its meat, make the sauce—all the day before—and you'll have only the actual soufflé mixture to complete before you pop the dish into the oven. Baking takes only 15 to 18 minutes, unsupervised.

Serving 6 people

The Lobster and Its Sauce Américaine:

Either one 2- to 2½-pound (1- to 1¼-kg) boiled lobster, or two or three 1-pound (450-g) lobsters (see directions at end of recipe)

4 Tb soft butter

2 to 3 Tb olive oil or fresh peanut oil

1 medium carrot, diced

1 medium onion, diced

⅓ cup (¾ dL) Cognac

1 cup (¼ L) lobster stock, fish stock, or chicken broth

½ cup (1 dL) beef stock or bouillon

1 cup (¼ L) dry white wine or dry white French vermouth

1½ cups (3½ dL) peeled, halved, and juiced tomatoes, chopped

2 to 4 Tb tomato paste or tomato sauce

1 tsp fragrant dried tarragon leaves

1 clove garlic, minced or puréed

Salt, pepper, and drops of hot pepper sauce

Beurre manié: 1½ Tb each flour and butter

Equipment:

A kettle, covered roaster, or steamer for cooking the lobsters; lobster shears are useful; a heavy large saucepan or casserole for simmering the shells

Because you will want the end section of the tail, the front part of the chest, and the claws for shell decoration, remove the lobster meat from the shells so as not to damage these parts (see illustrations, page 60). Discard sand sack and intestinal vein; scoop tomalley (green matter) and coral into a sieve set over a bowl. Rub through the sieve with the butter, scrape all residue off bottom of sieve into bowl, cover, and refrigerate, for enriching the finished sauce later. (Swish sieve into the sauce when it is boiling, to gather into the sauce all extra flavors.) Cut lobster meat into smallish pieces, the largest being about ½ inch (1½ cm); refrigerate until you are ready to bake the soufflé. Chop the shells (after reserving those for final decoration).

Film a large saucepan with oil, set over high heat, and when very hot add the chopped lobster shells. Stir and toss for 2 to 3 minutes, then add the diced carrot and onion, tossing and stirring for 2 minutes more. Pour in the Cognac, ignite with a lighted match, and let flame for several seconds, shaking the pan; extinguish with the stock, bouillon, and wine. Stir in the tomatoes, tomato paste, tarragon, garlic, ¼ teaspoon salt, pepper, and drops of hot pepper sauce. Cover and simmer 30 minutes, stirring up once or twice. Turn into a large sieve set over another saucepan; stir and shake sieve to loosen vegetables from shells. Then remove shells and press juices out of vegetables in sieve. (Reserve shells and vegetable residue.)

You should have about 1½ cups (3½ dL) of rosy-colored wine-flavored lobster juices, which will need a light thickening with *beurre manié* as follows: Blend the butter and flour into a paste, and whip into the hot lobster juices. Simmer, stirring with wire whip, for 2 minutes, and correct seasoning. (Sieved tomalley-butter will go in just before serving.) Refrigerate until you are ready to assemble the soufflé.

(Simmer reserved shells and vegetables in lightly salted water to cover for 25 to 30 minutes. Strain, and you will have a good lobster stock to put in your freezer.)

A savory lobster stock made from shells and aromatic vegetables

The Soufflé:

3 ½ Tb butter

6 croutons (rounds of crustless white bread sautéed in clarified butter, see page 110)

The lobster meat, sauce, tomalley, and shells

3 Tb flour

1 cup (¼ L) hot milk

½ tsp salt

⅛ tsp white pepper

⅔ cup egg whites (5 "large" whites or 1 ½ dL)

A pinch of salt

¼ tsp cream of tartar

3 egg yolks

¾ cup (1 ¾ dL) lightly pressed down, coarsely grated Swiss cheese

Equipment:

A large ovenproof platter, such as a shallow oval about 16 inches (40 cm) long; a very clean dry bowl and beater for the egg whites

Half an hour or so before you wish to bake the soufflé (which will take 15 to 18 minutes), you may prepare the platter: smear it with 1 tablespoon butter, arrange the croutons upon it, and divide the lobster meat over the croutons. Dribble ½ tablespoon of the lobster sauce over each portion of lobster. (Refrigerate the platter if you are not proceeding.)

Cheese Soufflé Base:

Preheat oven to 425°F/220°C. Prepare the rest of the ingredients listed. If egg whites are cold, pour into their beating bowl and set bottom of bowl in hot water, stirring the whites until they are just tepid to your finger—cold egg whites do not mount properly.

Heat 2½ tablespoons butter in a 2½-quart (2½-L) heavy-bottomed saucepan, and when melted stir in the flour; cook, stirring slowly until they foam and froth together for 2 minutes without coloring more than a buttery yellow. Remove from heat, and when this *roux* has stopped bubbling, vigorously beat in the hot milk with a wire whip and add the salt and pepper. Bring to the boil, stirring, for 1 minute. Remove from heat, clean sauce off sides of pan with a rubber spatula, and at once start in on the egg whites. Beat them at moderate speed until they start to foam, beat in the pinch of salt and cream of tartar; gradually increase speed to fast and continue beating until egg whites form stiff shining peaks when a bit is lifted up.

Immediately beat the 3 egg yolks into the hot sauce, then stir ¼ of the egg whites into the sauce (to lighten it). Scoop the rest of the egg whites onto the sauce and fold them together, alternating with sprinklings of cheese (but save 2 tablespoons for top of soufflé); operate deftly and rapidly so as to deflate the egg whites as little as possible.

Assembling and baking

Mound the soufflé over the lobster-topped croutons, topping each with a pinch of cheese. Bake immediately in the upper middle level of the preheated oven. Set timer for 15 minutes. Soufflé is done when nicely puffed and browned—it does not puff up like a soufflé in a dish, but rises at least 3 times its original volume. Tuck the shell and claws at one end of the platter, the tail at the other, and rush to the table.

While soufflé is baking, reheat sauce to the simmer, and correct seasoning; just before serving, remove from heat, whisk in the tomalley butter, and pour into a warm serving bowl. Surround each serving of soufflé with a ladleful of sauce.

Mounding the soufflé mixture over the lobster meat

A Remark on the Sauce:

Another trick for the sauce, after you have sautéed the shells and simmered them with wine and vegetables, is to remove the little legs, chop them, and purée them in a blender with a cup of the sauce. Then rub this through a sieve and back into the sauce, thus catching a little puréed lobster meat in there, to act as a light thickening. (I felt the recipe was long enough without adding this to it!)

To Boil or Steam Live Lobsters:

Whether to boil or steam lobsters is, I think, a question of personal preference, number of lobsters, and equipment. If you are to boil them you need a large enough pot to hold them, and a strong heat source that will bring the water rapidly back to the boil when the lobsters go in.

To boil them, plunge them headfirst and upside down into enough rapidly boiling water to submerge them; cover the pot and weight it down if necessary. As soon as the water comes back to the boil remove cover, and boil slowly but steadily until the time (below) is up.

To steam lobsters, place a rack in a kettle or roaster, add 1½ inches (4 cm) water, and bring to the boil. Place lobsters on rack, cover closely—weighting down cover if necessary to make a tight seal—and when water starts steaming, set your timer according to the following chart:

1 to 1¼ pounds 450 to 565 g	10–12 minutes
1½ to 2 pounds 675 to 900 g	15–18 minutes
2½ to 5 pounds 1¼ to 2¼ kg	20–25 minutes

When is the lobster done?

It is done when the meat will just separate from the shells, and when the tomalley inside the lobster has coagulated. But how can you

Head, claw, and tail shells announce that this is a soufflé of . . . lobster!

tell that without opening the lobster? I remove one of the little legs if I have any doubts; and if the leg meat is white and lobsterlike, I conclude the whole is cooked. Some experts can tell immediately by the look and feel of the underside of the tail section.

Removing the meat from a lobster

1) To separate the tail from chest, hold chest firmly with one hand and gently twist off tail with the other, drawing end of tail meat from chest.

2) Push tail meat out from the shell.

3) To remove intestinal vein or tube, cut a shallow slit down curve of tail meat, and pull it out—if you can see it.

4) Grab little legs, twist, and chest meat comes loose, along with legs, from chest shell.

5) Sand or stomach sac is inside chest cavity at the head; pull it out and discard it.

6) Delicious meat is in the chest interstices, but you have to dig it out bit by bit.

7) Bend the small claw down at right angles from the large claw and with it will come a large cartilage from the meat of the large claw. Then cut a window in the base of the large claw, and the meat can be removed in one piece. Dig the small sliver of meat out of the small claw.

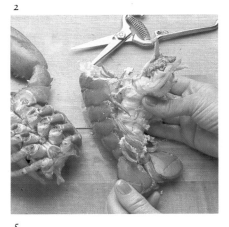

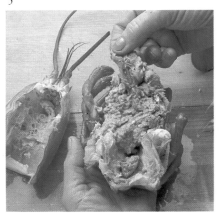

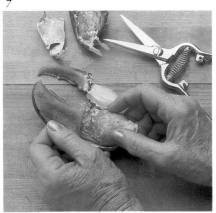

Salade Mimosa

Minced hard-boiled eggs and fresh green herbs tossed together do give a suggestion of flowering mimosa, that harbinger of spring along the Mediterranean. Sprinkle over a nicely seasoned tossed green salad and you have a very simple solution of how to dress it up for a party. Prepare the salad greens as usual—Boston lettuce or romaine seems best for this treatment. Mix the dressing (one of the vinaigrette choices on page 110). Hard boil 2 eggs and sieve or chop them (you might try the ingenious egg-slicer mincing technique on page 105) and mince enough fresh green herbs to make 2 to 3 table-spoons, using parsley, and chives, basil, or tarragon if you have them; toss herbs and eggs together in a small bowl with a sprin-kling of salt and pepper. Just before serving, toss the salad with the dressing, taste, and correct seasoning; toss lightly with half the egg and herb mixture, and sprinkle the rest of it on top.

A sprinkling of chopped egg and parsley dresses up greens.

Pumpernickel Melba

Thin toasted cheese-topped pumpernickel, or rye

Southern California spawns many unusual and/or original edibles, from salads and avo-cado ice cream to this savory version of crisp, waferlike toast served in many a Bev-erly Hills restaurant—a dusky Melba of pumpernickel or rye bread, sprinkled with cheese and sometimes herbs as it crisps. The only actual problem, besides being capable of slicing it almost paper thin, is that of finding storebought unsliced bread if you've none homemade. That, as we found in the pre-vious volume of *J.C. & Co.*, seems to be the ever-present Melba drawback.

For an unspecified amount

Stale unsliced pumpernickel or rye bread

Finely grated Parmesan cheese, or a mixture of hard cheeses like Cheddar, Swiss, etc.

Dried herbs, finely ground, such as oregano, thyme, or an herb mixture (optional)

Slice the bread as thin as possible, less than ⅛ inch (½ cm)—if it's not thin it will not curl as it bakes, the way Melba toast should. Lay the slices in one layer on a baking sheet or sheets, and place in a preheated 425 °F/ 220 °C oven. In 3 or 4 minutes, when bread has begun to crisp, sprinkle each slice with ½ teaspoon or so cheese and a pinch of the optional herbs. Continue baking a few min-utes more, until crisp and, you hope, some-what curled.

❷　Any leftovers may be packaged and frozen; warm again in the oven to crisp be-fore serving.

Pears Poached in White Wine

Compote de poires au vin blanc

A compote of fresh fruit seems a far more European than American dessert, yet it is so simple to do and delicious to eat that we should think of it more often. Also, it solves the problem of how to cope with those pears and peaches that are ripe and ready to eat, and won't keep another moment without spoiling: once compoted, they will keep well a goodly number of days in the refrigerator, ready to be served up as is, or dressed in all manner of plain or fancy ways.

The Poaching Syrup for Raw Fruits:
The proportions of sugar to liquid for poaching raw fruits are 6 tablespoons per cup of liquid, which makes 1½ cups sugar per quart (6 Tb per ¼ L; 3½ dL per L).

For 6 pears of the Anjou, Bartlett, Comice size

---

3 cups (¾ L) dry white wine or dry white French vermouth

---

1 cup (¼ L) water

The zest (yellow part of peel) of 1 lemon, and 4 Tb of its juice

---

1 stick or ½ tsp powdered cinnamon

1½ cups (3½ dL) sugar

---

6 firm ripe unblemished pears

Pears have cooked in their fragrant syrup.

If you are to poach the pears whole, as for this recipe (rather than halved or quartered as in many other recipes), you may not have enough liquid for 6 large pears to be submerged; in that case, either poach them in 2 batches or make more poaching syrup according to the proportions noted.

Choose a saucepan that will be large enough to hold the pears submerged in the syrup, place the syrup ingredients in the pan, and bring to the simmer; simmer 5 minutes (to bring out the various flavors into the liquid), then remove from heat.

One by one, with an apple corer or grapefruit knife, core the pears from the bottom—however, you may leave them uncored if you wish. Peel the pear neatly and drop at once into the syrup to prevent discoloration. When all pears are done, bring just to the simmer and maintain liquid at the not-quite-simmer for 8 to 10 minutes, until pears are tender through when pierced with the sharp point of a small knife. (Careful not to boil them, since that can break them apart.) When done, cover pan and leave the pears to absorb the flavors of the syrup for 20 minutes, or until you are ready to use them.

🕐   May be done several days in advance; cover and refrigerate them.

Serving suggestions
Serve the pears in an attractive bowl, along with their poaching syrup; you may wish to accompany them with heavy cream, lightly whipped cream, fresh strawberry or raspberry sauce, chocolate sauce, custard sauce. Or you may drain them, set them on a round of sponge cake or a macaroon that has been sprinkled with some of the poaching syrup and a few drops of Cognac or rum, then spoon sauce over them. Or serve them on vanilla ice cream or sherbet, and top with a chocolate, custard, or fruit sauce. Or combine them with other fruits and serve in a savarin. Or serve them in chocolate cups, as described here.

A Pear and Chocolate Dessert

Les délices aux poires

Whenever you have pears poached in wine, macaroons, chocolate cups, and caramel sauce all at hand at one moment, this lovely dessert is a fast assembly job. However, because the chocolate cups can soften and collapse in a warm room, and the caramel topping will lose its sheen as it gradually slides off the pears, you cannot assemble all of it ahead of time. You can set the pears in their chocolate cups well ahead, however, if you have room in the refrigerator to store them on their dessert plates, but the sauce should either go on at the last minute in the kitchen, or be spooned over each pear as you present it at the table.

Note: Directions for the chocolate cups, macaroons, and sauce follow this recipe.
For 6 people

6 chocolate cups
6 macaroons (optional)
Droplets of pear poaching liquid
Droplets of rum, Cognac, or bourbon whiskey (optional)
6 pears poached in white wine (preceding recipe)
About 1 cup (¼ L) caramel sauce

An hour or so before serving, if you wish to ready things ahead, set the chocolate cups on individual dessert plates. Choose, or trim, macaroons, if you are using them, to fit the bottom of the cups, and place them in upside down. Dribble over each a few drops of pear liquid and the optional rum, Cognac, or bourbon. Trim bottoms of pears if necessary, so they will sit solidly, and set the pears on the macaroons.

❷　Must be refrigerated at this point if prepared in advance.

Just before serving, or at the table, spoon a tablespoon or 2 of the caramel sauce over each pear.

Wine-poached pear, macaroon cushion, and chocolate cup

Chocolate Cups

*To hold ice creams and sherbets,
Bavarian creams, poached fruits*

*About 12 ounces or 2 cups (340 g or
½ L) chocolate bits or morsels for 6
chocolate cups*

Choose fluted paper cupcake molds of any
size you wish—the ones here have a 2¼-inch
(5¾-cm) bottom, and were bought in a local
supermarket. Because you want a wide cup
to hold the fruit, press out the flutings between your thumb and forefinger. Provide
yourself with several custard cups, shells,
small bowls, or large muffin tins in which to
set the chocolate-lined cups to congeal, later.

Then melt your chocolate—after numerous experiments we found chocolate bits
more satisfactory than semisweet bars—bits,
they say, have more viscosity, and that means
spreading ability, which you need for
this enterprise. To melt the chocolate, set it
in a smallish saucepan; bring another and
larger saucepan with about 2 inches (5 cm)
water to the boil, remove from heat and let
cool a moment, then cover the chocolate pan
and set it in the hot water. In 4 to 5 minutes
the chocolate bits will have melted; stir them
up and they should form a shining liquid
mass. (Be very careful not to use too much
heat here, or the chocolate will harden into a
lumpy or granular mess.)

Using the back of a teaspoon or a small
palette knife, spread the chocolate up the
sides of the cup, and in a layer on the bottom. Set each, as done, in a bowl or shell,
and refrigerate until set—15 to 20 minutes.
Carefully peel off the paper. Keep chilled
until you are ready to fill and serve them.

*Spread the melted chocolate up the sides of a fluted paper
cookie cup.*

Rosemary Manell's Almond Macaroons

Made in a food processor

My friend Rosie has conducted a good number of cooking classes featuring the food processor; this is the recipe for marvelous macaroons that she developed, and has kindly contributed. I've tried it in the blender without success; one could certainly adapt it to a large mortar and pestle in the time-honored hand-pounded way. But the processor is so quick and easy for macaroons that I've not gone into other methods seriously. By the way, Rosie prefers either Reese or "Red-E" almond paste, and brands of almond paste do vary in sweetness and consistency. Thus, if your first batch is too sweet, add less sugar the next time.

For 2 dozen macaroons 2 inches (5 cm) in diameter

8 ounces (225 g) almond paste
1 cup (¼ L) sugar
¼ tsp pure almond extract
A pinch of salt
¼ to ⅜ cup egg whites (2 to 3 whites; ½ to ¾ dL)

Equipment:
A food processor with steel blade; 2 baking sheets lined with brown paper (the shopping-bag kind); a pastry bag with ⅜-inch (1-cm) tube opening (optional)

Prepare cookie sheets, but do not grease them or grease the paper. Preheat oven to 325 °F/165 °C, and set racks in lower and upper middle levels.

Cut almond paste into ½-inch (1½-cm) pieces. Put into container of processor and cut up finely, turning motor on and off in 2-second spurts. When almond paste resembles coarse brown sugar, add the granulated sugar and process again in spurts, stopping several times to scrape down sides of container with a rubber spatula. Add the almond extract, salt, and ¼ cup (½ dL) egg whites, and process until no lumps of almond paste remain. The mixture should not be stiff, but should hold in a mass on a spatula. (If too stiff, add a little more egg white and process again.) This is the consistency for macaroons that are crunchy on the outside and chewy inside; if you like them softer and chewier, add more egg white by half teaspoons—after a batch or 2 you will arrive at the consistency you prefer.

Remove the mixture to a bowl and beat well with a wooden spoon, to be sure all is smooth and well blended. To form the macaroons, either drop mixture from a spoon, or use a pastry bag. If they are to fill chocolate cups, they should be small enough to fit inside easily: form ¾-inch (2-cm) blobs on the brown paper, spacing them 1½ inches (4 cm) apart because they spread a little as they bake. For larger macaroons, make the blobs 1½ inches (4 cm) across. Smooth tops of blobs with the back of a spoon dipped in cold water.

Bake in preheated oven for 25 to 30 minutes, switching sheets on the racks halfway through. The macaroons are done when lightly browned and crusty on top. Remove baking sheets from oven and let cool on cake racks. When cold, turn paper with macaroons attached upside down and dampen the back of the paper with a wet cloth or a brush; when macaroons loosen easily, peel away the paper. If they do not come off easily, dampen paper and wait a few minutes more. Set macaroons on cake racks for half an hour or so to dry.

❷ Store in an airtight tin, or wrap airtight and freeze.

▶ Remarks:
We tried forming and baking the macaroons on floured and buttered nonstick pastry sheets. They came off all right, but the bottoms were concave, and they were very crisp. Silicone baking paper was also unsatisfactory.

Caramel Sauce

This is a rich and pure caramel sauce that you can serve either hot or cold—it thickens as it cools. You can also combine it with whipped cream or custard sauce, or use as a base for caramel ice cream.

For about 1 cup or ¼ L

1 cup (¼ L) granulated sugar

⅓ cup (¾ dL) water

An additional ⅓ to ½ cup (¾ to 1 dL) water

1 cup (¼ L) heavy cream

Boil the sugar and ⅓ cup (¾ dL) water in a small heavy saucepan, swirling pan by its handle until sugar has completely dissolved and liquid is perfectly clear. Put a lid on the pan and boil slowly until sugar bubbles thicken considerably. Then uncover, and boil undisturbed for a moment or so, until syrup begins to caramelize. Immediately swirl pan slowly by its handle until syrup has turned a nice walnut brown. Remove from heat, swirling (if pan is very heavy, set bottom in cold water to stop the cooking) until bubbling has ceased. Avert your face, pour in the additional water, and simmer, stirring frequently, until caramel has melted into the water; boil down until it is a light syrup. Add the cream, blend in thoroughly, and boil, stirring, for 2 to 3 minutes, to reduce the cream slightly. Serve cold, for the pears.
🕐   May be made several days in advance; can be frozen, but may need boiling up and/ or more cream before using.

🕐 *Timing*

The pumpernickel Melba, the chocolate cups, and the macaroons can be made any time and frozen.

Buy your pears several days ahead, since they usually aren't sold ripe; if you do have ripe ones, you may poach them several days in advance. At this time, make the caramel sauce, and you can sauté and freeze the croutons for the soufflé.

The day before your party, you can prepare your lobsters and their sauce. The chocolate cups may be peeled and rechilled.

In the morning, prepare your salad, and store the lettuce wrapped in damp towels in the refrigerator. Prepare the vinaigrette.

An hour or so before your guests come, prepare the soufflé platter with its croutons and mounds of lobster meat; cover and refrigerate it.

Half an hour before serving time, make the soufflé, which takes only 15 to 18 minutes to bake. Assemble the dessert, except for the sauce. Crisp the pumpernickel Melba in the oven if you have made it early and frozen it.

The salad is tossed just before you serve it. Same for saucing the dessert, so that the caramel keeps its sheen.

Pumpernickel Melba

Menu Variations

The soufflé: as long as you have your fine lobster sauce, you can mix some fin fish with your lobster, like monkfish or halibut—this is an old Norwegian trick I learned when we were living there. The flavor of lobster is so strong and fine that it pervades other fish, too. You may use the same sauce system for live crabs and for fresh or frozen shrimp in the shell. You must be very careful with frozen shrimp, however, to be sure they have not been adulterated with preserving chemicals—I've run into some loathsome examples that really exude a smell like that of floor-cleaning fluid. Read the label on the package! Rather than shellfish and sauce *à l'américaine,* you could use sole poached in white wine, to flake over the croutons, and turn the poaching liquid into a *sauce au vin blanc*—a hollandaise made with the reduced white-wine fish stock. Another idea is to place a cold poached egg on each crouton, and a piece of ham or a dollop of cooked spinach on the crouton first, if you wish. When the soufflé is cooked, the egg has miraculously just warmed through; serve the soufflé with a hollandaise sauce, and you have a beautiful dish. (A recipe for the fish soufflé is in *The French Chef Cookbook,* as is a conventional, rather than platter, one for poached eggs and spinach.)

The salad: to follow a subtle soufflé, I'd always choose a salad on the delicate side—perhaps Rosie's spectacularly arranged lettuce salad on page 30, or a salad of Belgian endive (if it's affordable) with watercress. Something like a *salade niçoise* would be too much, as would most vegetable combinations—tomatoes especially, since they'd repeat the sauce *à l'américaine.* You could certainly serve pita bread triangles, toasted and cheesed, instead of the *pumpernickel Melba.*

The dessert: apples, peaches, etc., could be poached in the same way as the pears and used instead. Rather than chocolate cups, you could use vacherin meringue cases, or cookie cups. (A recipe for the latter is in *The French Chef Cookbook.*) Other fruit sauces are very easy to make: use frozen strawberries or raspberries and purée in a blender or processor, adding fresh lemon juice and more sugar as needed. For fresh berries, purée, beating in lemon juice and sugar to taste; raspberries need sieving, I think.

Leftovers

Little to say here! Any cook who would not promptly devour the last scrap of leftover lobster meat must be certifiably mad. Other uses for poached fruit and chocolate cases are in the recipes themselves. As for caramel sauce, who needs telling?

Postscript: Lunch or luncheon?

If you are requesting the pleasure of Mr. and Mrs. John Doe's company then you call it "luncheon." The added syllable gives extra employment to needy engravers, I guess, and anyway the word seems nicely old-fashioned to me. It does make one stop and think about menu planning for formal entertainment nowadays, when "tummy time," as Winston Churchill called his interior clock, has been reset by the press of our obligations.

Except on holidays, few of us can take our time at midday, whereas a dinner party can sprawl on into the wee hours. (Do we admit to sleeping off lunch?) If you and your guests are coring the heart out of a busy day, and devoting it to a meal that so many people are apt to skip or skimp, you are declaring an Occasion. A modern lunch*eon* menu should be light, and as compact and elegant as a sonnet. It is a good time to focus on one artful and unusual dish. And, since at midday people (a) come on time, and (b) don't want much to drink, you are secure in planning something that won't wait, like fish, or a grill, or a soufflé. No wonder so many enthusiastic cooks rise, like the sun, to their zenith at this hour.

"Love in a cold climate" is the phrase for these hearty, comforting dishes from Down East. Great food when a gale is howling outside.

New England Potluck Supper

Menu

New England Fresh Fish Chowder

❧

Cole Slaw

❧

*Indian Pudding with
Vanilla Ice Cream or Custard Sauce*

❧

*Suggested wines:
Cider, beer, or dry white wine*

You would think every northern region of the world would have a version of New England chowder: salt pork and potatoes and onions are everywhere, to combine with whatever fresh or salt fish—or even vegetables—might be handy. But it isn't so: chowder is as typical of New England as the Down East accent which pronounces it to rhyme with "howdah." Equally typical is Indian pudding, so called because it is based on "Indian Meal," the ground dried corn which the early settlers obtained from the Indians of the Bay Colony.

Born a Californian, I first tasted Indian pudding as an adult. It was made by—of all people—an Armenian chef in a restaurant in Lexington, Massachusetts. I loved that first Indian pudding. It was hearty and rich and elemental, deep in flavor, in texture almost like caramel, and I felt it was born out of a harsh climate and an economy of scarcity. I can't taste Indian pudding without thinking of it simmering all of an iron-hard January afternoon, slowly releasing its comfortable spicy scent into a cold dark little cabin. It must have hit the spot for frozen weary people who'd been hacking all day at the endless forest. Chowder, on the other hand, has a summery quality to me, perhaps because I associate it with July and August in Maine, with salty sun-baked granite around me and the sea crinkling below—and with the knowledge that a pail of wild berries is waiting in a cool purple cranny in the rocks. But it's a great dish any time, and a hearty one.

The name comes from *chaudière,* French for the big iron cauldron which was an all-purpose cooking vessel in early times. It could be hung from a fireplace crane, or, if of the footed type, be stood in the warm embers. We borrowed a beautiful old one from the ancient Wayside Inn at Sudbury, Massachusetts, for our television show on chowder, as well as showing forth some machines for grinding your own Indian pudding corn. Of course you can make chowder in any old pot, and of course you can buy cornmeal anywhere; it doesn't make much difference. But I wanted to make a point of the earthy, primal simplicity of these great American dishes. There are loads of recipes around for both fish chowder and Indian pudding, and many cooks insist their particular recipes are the only authentic versions; but the ones I'm giving here are the ones I like, so for me they're the best, the most gen-

uine, indeed the only recipes worth cooking. I like my chowder with untraditional trimmings: croutons instead of pilot biscuits, and sour cream and parsley instead of a final blob of butter. My Indian pudding version is severely plain—unusual, though, in that it contains grated apple; but in fact it's a very old version.

It is adapted from the recipe of Lydia Maria Child (no relation to me), an early feminist of stern and rockbound character, who never, I suspect, threw away a scrap of paper or string and whose mission in life was to teach us all how to live sparely. Her book *The American Frugal Housewife* was first published in 1829, and went through many editions. (A facsimile of the twelfth, published in 1971, is available through the Office of Educational Services, Ohio State University Libraries, Columbus, Ohio 43210.) Mrs. Child's recipe for pudding involves long slow baking and two applications of milk, stirred in the first time, floated on top the second. The result is rich, redolent, and guaranteed to stick to your ribs. There are versions with eggs, or versions cooked quickly; but they don't have that primeval New England Puritan quality that I find so appealing in Lydia Maria Child.

In their journals and in letters home, the settlers gave touchingly fervent thanks for the variety of fish, game, and wild berries they found in New England; but they hadn't much choice of ingredients that kept well. Maybe, if put to it, some goodwives occasionally had to use salt pork, onions, and molasses twice in the same meal. Mercifully, we don't, so my excellent recipe for authentic-tasting baked beans, adapted to modern methods, is not suggested for this menu, but placed at a discreet distance, as a bonus.

Lydia Maria Child

Preparations

Marketing and Storage:
Staples to have on hand

Salt, regular and coarse or kosher (which is
    optional)
Peppercorns
Herbs and spices: sage or thyme; imported bay
    leaves; caraway or cumin seed;
    powdered ginger ▼

Wine vinegar
Mustard (the strong Dijon type)
Flour
Sugar
Butter
Eggs
Lemons
Celery, carrots, scallions, purple onion, green
    pepper
Fresh parsley

Specific ingredients for this menu

Fish: Several fish frames, if available, for fish
    stock, or bottled or canned clam
    juice (16 ounces or ½ L)
Fresh fish (2½ pounds or 1¼ kg), or see recipe
    for details ▼
Dark unsulphured molasses (½ cup or 1 dL)
Pure vanilla extract
Cornmeal (¼ cup or ½ dL), preferably stone
    ground ▼
Nonsweet white bread, for croutons
Milk (2 quarts or 2 L)
Sour cream (1 pint or ½ L) for chowder and
    cole slaw
Homemade mayonnaise (⅓ to ½ cup or 1 dL),
    optional for cole slaw
Fat-and-lean salt pork (6 ounces or 180 g) ▼
"Boiling" potatoes (4 pounds or 1¾ kg)
Onions (1½ pounds or 675 g or 6 medium-
    size)
Cabbage (1 small-medium)
Vanilla ice cream
Heavy cream
Tart apples (2 medium-size)

► *Remarks:*

Staples

Powdered ginger: you can season Indian pudding with a variety of spices, including cinnamon, nutmeg, allspice—alone or in combination—all of which the Puritans could get from the Caribbean Islands along with their molasses and their rum. But I like ginger alone, mostly for its taste but also for its eighteenth-century association with blue-and-white jars and the tall ships of the China trade.

Specific ingredients for this menu

Cornmeal: can be yellow or white, and I prefer it to be stone ground or home ground, although when it is cooked so long and with such strong flavors the regular supermarket kind is permissible. *Salt pork:* since this is an essential chowder ingredient it should be of top quality; I either use my own, or look and feel around in the supermarket display until I find a nice softish piece, meaning it is quite freshly salted. The blanching of the pork, in the recipe, not only removes excess salt but freshens the taste. *Fish:* certainly the beauty of a chowder resides in the quality of its fish, which must smell and taste as fresh as possible. The clam-juice substitute for your own fresh fish stock is acceptable, although it cannot compare in beauty of taste to the real thing.

New England Fresh Fish Chowder

For 6 people, as a main course

Either—2 or more large meaty fish frames (head and bone structure of freshly filleted fish) from cod, hake, haddock, sea bass, or other lean fish (to provide fish meat and fish stock)

Or—2½ pounds (1¼ kg) fresh cod, hake, haddock, or other lean fish fillets, all one kind or a mixture, plus either 4 cups (1 L) fish stock, or 2 cups (½ L) bottled or canned clam juice and 2 cups (½ L) water

6 ounces (180 g) fat-and-lean salt pork (rind off), diced into ⅜-inch (1-cm) pieces and blanched (boiled 5 minutes in 2 quarts or liters water and drained)

About 4½ cups (1 L) sliced onions

3 Tb flour (optional, but I like a light liaison here)

About 5 cups (1¼ L) sliced "boiling" potatoes

½ tsp sage or thyme

2 imported bay leaves

¼ tsp peppercorns, roughly crushed

Salt (coarse or kosher preferred) and pepper

Fish stock, milk, or water as necessary

½ cup (1 dL), or more, sour cream

⅓ cup (¾ dL) roughly chopped parsley

2 cups (½ L) toasted croutons tossed in butter, salt, and pepper

Equipment

A pressure cooker, optional

Fish stock from fish frames

If you are using fish frames, remove gills (the feathery red tissue) from head and whack fish into pieces that will fit into a kettle; cover with cold water, salt lightly, and boil 3 to 4 minutes or until meat is just cooked on bones. Scrape meat from bones and reserve; return remains to kettle and boil 20 minutes, then strain, discarding bones; this liquid is your fish stock.

The chowder base

Sauté the blanched salt pork several minutes in a 3-quart (3-L) saucepan (or bottom of pressure cooker), to brown very lightly and render fat. Stir in onions and cook 8 to 10 minutes, stirring frequently, until tender and lightly browned (or pressure-cook 2 minutes and release pressure). Drain out fat. Stir in optional flour, adding a little rendered pork fat if too dry, and cook slowly, stirring, for 2 minutes; remove from heat. Bring fish stock or clam juice and water to the simmer, then vigorously beat 4 cups (1 L) into the onions and pork; add the potatoes, herbs, and peppercorns, but no salt until potatoes are tender (or pressure-cook 2 minutes, release pressure, then simmer slowly 5 minutes to bring out flavors). Correct seasoning; you wait until now to add salt because salt pork may still be a bit salty, and storebought clam juice, if you used it, is bound to be.

🕐 May be completed in advance to this point; refrigerate, and cover when chilled. Will keep 2 days.

Finishing the chowder

Shortly before you are ready to serve, bring chowder base to the simmer. If you are using fresh fish, cut into 2-inch (5-cm) chunks and add to the chowder base along with additional stock, or milk, to cover ingredients; simmer about 5 minutes or until fish is just cooked—opaque rather than translucent and lightly springy. Do not overcook. If you are using cooked fish-frame meat, simply add it when chowder is at the simmer, along with more stock or milk, if you wish; it needs only warming through. Taste carefully and correct seasoning.

🕐 May be completed, chilled, then brought to a simmer again just before serving. Or you may keep the chowder warm for 20 minutes or so, loosely covered and set on an electric hot plate.

To serve

Ladle into wide soup plates, top with a dollop of sour cream, a sprinkling of parsley, and a handful of croutons.

Cole Slaw

For a low-calorie version, simply omit the mayonnaise and/or the sour cream (the liquid from the vegetables makes a natural dressing). Or, as a compromise, include the sour cream but pass a bowl of mayonnaise separately.

4 cups (1 L) thinly shredded cabbage
½ cup (1 dL) each diced green pepper, diced celery, grated carrot, minced scallions or purple onion
1 small apple, grated
3 Tb fresh minced parsley
2 Tb each wine vinegar and fresh lemon juice
1 Tb Dijon-type prepared mustard
1½ tsp each salt and sugar
2 pulverized imported bay leaves
½ tsp caraway or cumin seed
⅓ to ½ cup (¾ to 1 dL) homemade mayonnaise, or sour cream, or a mixture (optional)

Toss together the cabbage, vegetables, apple, and parsley. Combine the other ingredients to make dressing; toss with the cabbage mixture, taste carefully, correct seasoning, and toss again. Taste again; cover and refrigerate for several hours.

Indian Pudding

For about 6 cups, serving 6 to 8 people
Cooking time: 5 to 6 hours

¼ cup (½ dL) cornmeal, stone ground recommended
2 cups (½ L) cold milk, regular or low-fat
2 to 3 Tb butter or chopped fresh beef suet
1 tsp salt
2 tsp fragrant powdered ginger
Scant ½ cup (1 dL) excellent dark unsulphured molasses
1 tart apple, peeled, cored, and coarsely grated (scant 1 cup or ¼ L)
1 cup (¼ L) additional milk
To serve with the pudding: vanilla ice cream, or lightly whipped and sweetened cream, or Custard Sauce (see recipe), or heavy cream and sugar
Equipment
Corn grinder (see right)

Place the cornmeal in a heavy-bottomed 2-quart (2-L) saucepan and with a wire whip gradually beat in the milk. (Old recipes say to sprinkle cornmeal into boiling milk; do it this way if you prefer, but I find no need for it.) Set over moderately high heat and add the butter, salt, ginger, and molasses. Bring to the boil, stirring and beating with a wire whip to be sure all is smooth, then add grated apple. Boil 10 to 15 minutes, stirring frequently, until you have a thick, porridgelike mixture. Meanwhile, preheat oven to 350°F/180°C.

🕐 This preliminary cooking may be done ahead; set aside or refrigerate, and bring to the boil again before proceeding.

Turn the hot pudding mixture into a buttered 2-quart (2-L) baking dish and set uncovered in the middle level of the preheated oven for 20 minutes, or until bubbling. Stir up the pudding, blend in ½ cup (1 dL) additional milk, clean sides of dish with a rubber spatula, and turn oven down to 250°F/130°C. Bake 1½ to 2 hours longer.

Stir up again as before, and pour over surface of the pudding the remaining ½ cup (1 dL) milk, letting it float on top. Continue baking uncovered another 3 to 4 hours; the top will glaze over.

🕐 If you are not ready to serve by that time, cover the pudding and keep it warm, but not too hot or it will dry out.

Serve the pudding (which will look like a very thick caramel-brown sauce) warm, with the ice cream, whipped cream, the following sauce, or cream and sugar passed separately.

Custard Sauce (optional):

For 2 cups or ½ liter

Gradually beat 5 Tb sugar into 4 egg yolks and continue beating until mixture is pale yellow and forms the ribbon. By dribbles beat in 1 cup (¼ L) boiling milk. Set over moderately low heat and stir slowly with a wooden spoon, reaching all over bottom of pan and watching carefully as mixture slowly thickens: at first bubbles will appear on surface, and as they begin to disappear custard is about to thicken; a wisp of steam rising from the surface is another indication. Stir more rapidly, and as soon as custard lies in a creamy layer on the back of the spoon, it is done. Immediately remove from heat, stirring vigorously to cool. Beat in a tablespoon of unsalted butter and tablespoon of pure vanilla extract. Serve hot, warm, or cool.

🕐 May be made a day or two in advance and reheated carefully by stirring over hot water. May be frozen.

① *Timing*

There is only one last-minute job in this menu: adding the fish to the chowder 5 minutes before you serve it. That's for A-Plus results. But there are alternatives, none of which gets less than A-Minus. You can keep chowder warm; you can reheat it; you can make the "base" 2 days in advance. Note—start early if you are using the salt fish suggested in the following variations: 2 or 3 days to soak a whole fish, depending on its size; 24 hours or more for packaged salt cod; a few hours for chopped or shredded salt cod.

Cole slaw must, of course, be made and chilled in advance: anywhere between a few hours to 2 days.

Indian pudding is prepared half a day before serving, since its cooking time is 5 or 6 hours. It can, of course, be made in advance and reheated over hot water; but then you will probably lose the glazed crust because you will need to stir it as it warms.

Menu Variations

The chowder: Using the traditional chowder base of salt pork, onions, and potatoes, you can vary the recipe in a number of ways. You might like to use frozen fish or soaked salt codfish instead of fresh fish, with a fish stock. Vegetarians could make a hearty main course of corn chowder, using butter for salt pork and fresh cream-style grated corn. I wouldn't use such delicate, expensive shellfish as lobster or crab; but you could have scallops or mussels, and certainly clams. For mussels or steamer clams, because they can be terribly salty, I always soak them an hour or more in several changes of cold water. Then steam them open with ½ inch (1½ cm) water in a covered kettle; the steaming liquid becomes the chowder stock, and the shellfish meat, now fully cooked, goes into the finished chowder. Since hard-shelled clams can be tough, I steam them open, chop the meat, and cook it until tender with the pork and onions. As to other chowder systems, some cooks thicken their chowders by running one-quarter of the cooked potatoes through the blender with a little stock and returning them to the pot before the fish goes in. Some garnish chowder with extra bits of fried salt pork, chips of onions fried till dry and brown, or chopped chives. It's all good, and, providing you stick to the traditional base, it's all chowder.

Cole slaw: This splendid stuff has almost as many variations as it does aficionados, as a tour through the basic cookbooks amply illustrates. There's another good cole slaw, based on my friend Avis DeVoto's version, in *J.C.'s Kitchen.*

Indian pudding: "Maybe it's sacrilege," says Anthony Athanas of the Boston waterfront restaurant Anthony's Pier 4, "but we use raisins." For a light, eggy Indian pudding, you couldn't do better than his: ½ cup (1 dL) light cream is brought to the simmer in a double boiler with 2½ cups (6 dL) whole milk; you then add 3½ tablespoons cornmeal and 4 tablespoons granulated sugar, whisking as you go, and let simmer while you beat together 3 "extra-large" eggs, 2½ tablespoons brown sugar, 4 tablespoons molasses, a good pinch each cinnamon and ginger, a pinch nutmeg, and a small pinch salt. Add the heated milk and cream, blend completely, and stir in 5 tablespoons raisins; then pour into a baking dish, set in a pan containing 1 inch (2½ cm) boiling water, and bake for 2 hours at 400°F/200°C.

Leftovers, or:
Use it up, wear it out,
make it do,
or do without

Fish chowder: A completed chowder is good reheated and maybe frozen (once). In some thrifty New England households, part of the liquid is drained off and the solids are topped with buttered crumbs and baked until golden brown. The "base," with the stock added or not, is versatile indeed (see Menu Variations) and may be frozen. Extra fish stock, well strained and frozen, is a kitchen staple for sauces and soups. A very Yankee way of using extra cooked fish is to moisten it with cream or with a "cream" sauce (as they call it although it's usually creamless; the French would call it

Fish cakes and baked beans with English muffins

béchamel if the liquid is milk, or *velouté* if it is stock) and bake it topped with crumbs or pastry; "fish pie" is a Sunday-night staple Down East, and very good if you add a bit of crab or lobster, dry Madeira, and a speck of nutmeg. Leftover salt cod and potatoes make deep-fried fish cakes (eaten with baked beans on Sunday morning), or, mixed with thick white sauce and crumbed, it becomes fish croquettes. If you made your chowder with smoked fish, it's not far to finnan haddie for a second round. If you used clams, and have a few too many, steam extra raw soft-shelled ones and eat with melted butter; or steam open the hard-shelled type, chop the meat and mix with crumbs, season highly, stuff in the shells, and bake. Or save the soft-shelled type, which, raw and unopened, keep for 3 days in the refrigerator, and use them in a paella. (Steamer clams have rubbery black necks, which make them unappealing raw.) I really don't see much future (except reheating) for the remains of a corn chowder; but extra raw cream-style corn is a treasure not to be wasted.

Cole slaw: A completed cole slaw will keep for several days, though you will want to drain its accumulated juices after a while. You wouldn't want to shred extra cabbage unless you planned to use it soon, because the cut edges wilt, though iced water helps. Cabbage wedges, however, are integral to a New England boiled dinner. Quickly boiled, shredded cabbage is nice with butter and a few caraway or poppy seeds. Braised, with chestnuts or apples, or with sausage and salt meat (as in a *choucroute garnie*), it is delicious. You can bake it with tomato sauce, or with cream or cheese or bits of ham or bacon; you can stuff a strudel with it; or, perhaps best of all, you can combine it with leeks and potatoes for a hearty peasant soup. Or you can save a few outside leaves and stuff them (see *Mastering I*).

Indian pudding: It can be eaten cold or it can be reheated—best done in a double boiler.

Postscript: Another way to bake beans

A few summers ago a friend of ours on the coast of Maine dug a deep hole in his back yard and lined it with big round rocks. Then, one early morning, he built a fire in it and let it smoulder for several hours, raked coals out from the center, and put in a big iron pot filled with pork and beans. He raked the coals back over the pot, piled seaweed on top, and covered that with a canvas tarpaulin which he anchored in place with more big round rocks. In a few hours we could smell those beans cooking, and at 7 o'clock in the evening he unloosed the tarp, raked the seaweed and coal ash from around the pot, and lifted it out, its hoop-shaped handle grasped by a hook-and-pulley contraption he had constructed over the bean hole. We sat out on the grass, in a circle, while he lifted the lid to release the aroma of those slow-cooked beans with the flavor of onions, molasses, and pork baked right into them. They were almost crusty although surrounded by thick juices, and we ate them with great helpings of cole slaw and homemade rye bread.

I thought to myself at the time that I loved the idea of the bean hole, and I loved the beans that came out of it, but why wouldn't an electric Crock-Pot give the same effect? While not quite the same, as I found from experiment, it does produce an easy-cooking meal of pork and beans, and to make things even more untraditional I precooked the beans in a pressure cooker. Anyway, as with a fish chowder, there is no set recipe for baked beans, from Fannie Farmer, Mrs. Rorer, Lydia Maria Child, and on up to the old Boston restaurant of Durgin-Park. All the recipes have beans and pork, of course, but in differing quantities; some have molasses, or brown sugar, or even honey or maple syrup. Others include mustard, and vinegar, and tomato, while some have no onion at all, and so forth. I have therefore seasoned my beans to my own taste, which means more onions than usual, a little garlic, herbs, molasses, tomato, and mustard.

Manufacturing Notes:

The Crock-Pot, I find, is slow on cooking raw vegetables; thus I recommend precooking the onions separately with the pork before adding them to the beans. The beans themselves need precooking before they go in, and if they are not quite soft enough beforehand they may remain a little too crunchy even after several hours of crockery. As to the pork, I prefer to blanch it before cooking, to get rid of its salt; otherwise it can oversalt the beans. And whether or not to leave the pork whole or sliced is up to you; I like it cut into strips so that it distributes its considerable charms throughout the beans. Finally, if you don't have a Crock-Pot, just cook the beans in a casserole or bean pot in a 275°F/140°C oven, and if you've no pressure pan for the precooking, simmer the soaked beans in an open pot.

Baked Beans or Boston Baked Beans or Pork and Beans

*For about 2 quarts baked beans,
serving 6 people*

1 pound (450 g) small white beans

6 cups (1½ L) water (more if needed)

8 ounces (225 g) fat-and-lean salt pork (rind included)

2 cups (½ L) diced onions (2 medium-size onions)

2 large cloves garlic, minced or puréed

¼ cup (½ dL) each: dark molasses, plain tomato sauce or purée, and Dijon-type prepared mustard

1 Tb minced fresh ginger (optional)

1 imported bay leaf

½ tsp dried thyme, or mixed herbs such as Italian or Provençal blend

1½ tsp salt

Quick soaking and precooking of the beans

Toss the beans in a sieve and pick over carefully to remove any tiny stones (I found 14 in a box of beans the other day!), rinse under cold water, and place in pressure pan (or saucepan) with the 6 cups (1½ L) water. Bring rapidly to the boil and boil uncovered exactly 2 minutes; remove from heat, cover pan, and let sit exactly 1 hour. Then cover with lid and pressure valve and bring rapidly to full pressure for exactly 1 minute; set aside for 10 minutes, then release pressure (or simmer an hour or so in partially covered saucepan until beans are almost tender when you eat several as a test).

The pork, onions, and other ingredients

Meanwhile cut the salt pork into slices (including rind) ⅜ inch (1 cm) thick and, if you wish, cut the slices into sticks; drop into 2 quarts (2 L) cold water and simmer 10 minutes, then drain. Sauté for several minutes in a heavy-bottomed 10-inch (25-cm) frying pan until they start rendering some fat, then fold in the onions. Cover and cook over moderately low heat for 10 minutes or so, stirring up several times, until onions are quite tender but not browned. While onions are cooking, measure out the rest of the ingredients into the Crock-Pot (or a 3-quart or 3-L casserole).

Assembling and baking the beans

When the beans are done, drain them in a colander set over a bowl, and turn them into the Crock-Pot (or casserole), folding them together with the pork and onions and other ingredients. Pour in bean-cooking juices just to level of beans, adding additional water if you need more liquid. Cover Crock-Pot and set at "high" until contents are bubbling, usually 30 minutes, then cook at "low" for 6 to 8 hours, or until you feel the beans are done. (Or set casserole of beans in a 350°F/180°C oven for ½ hour or until bubbling, then turn oven down to 275°F/140°C and bake for 6 to 8 hours.) As they cook, the beans turn a brownish red—a more pronounced color in the oven than in the Crock-Pot—and the various flavors meld themselves into the beans while the juices thicken; their point of doneness is up to you.

🕐   May be baked several days in advance; let cool uncovered, then cover and chill. Reheat to bubbling either in Crock-Pot or in a casserole in a 325°F/170°C oven, and if they seem dry, add spoonfuls of water.

For families who like to cook and eat together, this homey, savory menu starts from the ground up with jobs for all ages.

Sunday Night Supper

Menu

Ivan's Apéritif

❧

*Corned Beef and Pork Boiled Dinner with
Steamed Vegetables
Cream of Garlic Sauce with Horseradish
Fresh Tomato Fondue—Diced tomatoes
simmered in herbs and oil*

❧

Homemade Noodles

❧

Sherbet with Strawberries en Chemise

❧

*Suggested wines:
Red Beaujolais or Zinfandel, beer, cider, milk*

Take 1 cup (140 g) flour, add enough salt to render it unappetizing, and blend in vegetable dye by droplets, kneading with enough water to form a stiff, elastic dough. Yield: 2 good fistfuls, depending on age. Keeps well in a wide-mouthed screw-top jar. Some cookbook this is; but I mention play dough, the toddler's joy, to remind you of the deep satisfaction we all, even babies, derive from kneading and manipulating dough. In the Child clan, we like to save Sunday night for a do-it-yourself family cooking bee; and anyone old enough to stay up is welcome. The most popular project with all ages is noodle-making-and-eating; all the more so since Paul and I acquired a thrifty, efficient little hand-cranked machine which makes lumps into sheets and then into ribbons— wavy, pale-gold strips a yard long which are briefly dried over a broomstick suspended between two chairs. At table the younger members learn, by practicing it, the small, gratifying art of eating noodles deftly: the fork, held vertically to the plate, engages a few strands with the tines and rotates against the inside of a spoon, making a neat parcel. Decorum reigns, unless Paul elects to demonstrate noodle eating as we learned it in China during World War II. I am sorry to say that his deafening inhalations are widely copied.

However you eat them, noodles are not only amusing but delicious—and almost universal, as you discover in any wheat-growing corner of the world. Just how delicious, you won't discover until you make your own. The machine does practically all the kneading and all the rolling and cutting. It's a pleasure to use, and we all take turns cranking it and catching the ribbons as they fall from the cutters. Homemade noodles have a lovely nutty flavor and a tender texture. They cook in half the time of storebought noodles and cost precisely half as much. We reckoned it out that the compact, well-built machine had paid for itself after 76 two-egg batches ... rather soon, in other words, since people borrow it constantly.

Noodles are good with almost anything, but once or twice a year Paul and I start well in advance and corn our own meat for a Sunday party. I suppose this sounds like reinventing the wheel! Meat used to be corned (salted and spiced) in order to preserve it, which in these days of refrigeration is unnecessary; and, if you do like corned beef, you can buy it anywhere. But we like corned pork sometimes (which you can't often buy); we prefer short-fibered cuts to the usual brisket; and, finally, we fancy our own combinations of spices and

the appetizing light-brown color of meat corned without nitrates (potassium salts) to turn it commercial red. Before refrigerators, the process was cumbersome: you needed a big stone crock with a lid fitting inside it like a piston in a cylinder; weights for the lid; and, most important, a cold room or outbuilding where the temperature stayed at 37°F/3°C. But this is usual refrigerator temperature, and a plastic bag works just as well as a crock—provided you remember to massage the package daily for a minute or two. (Using a crock, you didn't have to do that, since the meat was surrounded with brine; in a bag, the salt and meat juices create a brine, but you have to be sure it cures the meat on all sides.)

While the meat is cooking and the noodles are being kneaded, extruded, draped, and dried, other pairs of hands are preparing a bouquet of beautifully trimmed vegetables for the steamer. And the smallest hands are at work on a decoration for our dessert of storebought strawberry sherbet or ice cream, a soft fresh flavor to round off a savory dinner. The makings are a tray of plump strawberries with a bowl of quickly prepared royal icing to dip them in; it clothes each berry in a little white velvet shirt—hence the name *en chemise.* A few strawberries always seem to disappear at this stage—which is only fair, since we elders are sipping away as we putter. There are fresh tomatoes to be peeled, seeded, juiced, and chopped, and a pot to be watched as the pale, subtle cream of garlic sauce is reduced and a touch of horseradish added.

Since we are, after all, busy accomplishing something, our drink is a mild one, something I first tasted in California. With its mixed vermouths and the light filming of gin (not for kick, but for flavor and satiny flow), it's finely, richly aromatic. And lovely to behold. Properly served in a big goblet of ice, with a goldfish-sized curve of orange zest, it looks so full and glowing that I wonder if my brother-in-law, who invented it, was inspired by the California sunset. Anyway, the family has named it Ivan's Apéritif for him, and we always like to have it together on the night that rounds off the week.

Preparations

Recommended Equipment:

For corning the meats, you'll need sturdy plastic bags with fasteners, a large bowl with a plate or pan that fits inside it, and a 10-pound (5-kg) weight to set on it.

For making noodles, a hand-cranked pasta machine (which also makes lasagne and thin noodles) is desirable. The electric models are at least five times the price and are supposed to be good, but I've never tried one.

To cook dinner, you'll need three big pots, at least two of them with well-fitting lids, and a metal colander which fits one of the pots—or, preferably, use a steaming rack.

Marketing and Storage:

If you are going to do the corned meats for this menu, you'll need to start two weeks in advance, so I have marked the items for corned meat making with an asterisk on the list.

Staples to have on hand

Table salt
*Coarse or kosher salt
*Black and white peppercorns
*Powdered spices and herbs: allspice, thyme,
    sage, paprika, bay leaf
*Optional: juniper berries
 Whole cloves
 Whole imported bay leaves
 Prepared white horseradish
 Olive oil
*Granulated sugar
 Confectioners sugar
 Cornstarch
 Flour
 Eggs (about 6 "large")
 Butter
 Heavy cream (1 cup or ¼ L)
*Garlic (2 heads)
 Parsley
 Optional: chives
 Shallots and/or scallions
 Lemons (2)
 Oranges (2)
 Cognac
 Gin

Specific ingredients for this menu

*Beef and/or pork, braising cut (see recipe)
*Carrots
 White turnips (at least 3 or 4)
*Rutabaga (1 large)
*Onions and/or leeks
 Celery
 Optional: green beans (1 pound or 450 g)
 Tomatoes (8 to 10)
 Strawberries (24 large)
 Strawberry sherbet or ice cream (2 quarts
    or liters)
 Sweet white French or Italian vermouth
 Dry white French vermouth
 Optional: milk, cider, apple juice

Ivan's Apéritif

Mixed vermouth with orange

Ingredients per drink

1 jigger dry white French vermouth (Noilly Prat, Martini & Rossi, or Boissière)

1 jigger sweet white vermouth (Cinzano, Gancia, Lillet, or white Dubonnet)

1 Tb gin

1 fresh zest of orange (a 2½-inch or 6-cm strip of the orange part of the peel)

Equipment

A large, clear, stemmed wineglass; ice cubes

Fill the wineglass with ice cubes, stir in the vermouths, float the gin on top but do not stir in, squeeze the zest over the glass, then rub the rim of the glass with it and drop the zest into the glass.

A Junior Version:

For the vermouths and the gin, substitute apple juice or cider. The orange zest, the big glass, and the ice are the important parts.

Corned Beef and Pork

Potted, salted, and/or spiced meat— home cured in plastic bags rather than in a crock or pot

Salt and Spice Mixture:
For 10 to 12 pounds or 4½ to 5½ kg meat

1⅓ cups (3¼ dL) coarse or kosher salt

3 Tb granulated sugar

1 Tb cracked peppercorns

2 tsp each powdered allspice and thyme

1 tsp each powdered sage, paprika, and bay leaf

Special Optional Aromatic
Vegetable Mixture for Beef:
For 4 to 5 pounds or 2 to 2½ kg meat

½ cup (1 dL) each: minced rutabaga, onion, and carrot

2 large cloves garlic, minced

Special Optional Addition for Pork:
For 4 to 5 pounds or 2 to 2½ kg meat

2 Tb crushed juniper berries

The Meat—One Kind or Cut,
or a Mixture:

Beef: brisket, chuck, eye round roast, bottom round

Brisket

Pork: shoulder arm picnic or blade (butt); loin, blade end (bone-in or boneless for either shoulder or loin)

Equipment

Sturdy plastic bags, one for each piece of meat; secure fastenings for bags; a large bowl or other receptacle to hold meat; a plate or pan to cover meat; a 10-pound (5-kg) weight to set in plate or pan; washed cheesecloth

Curing the meat

Trim meat of excess fat (and bone it, if you wish, but do not tie it until the curing is finished). Blend the salt and spice mixture in a bowl, set the meat on a tray, and rub mixture into all sides of meat and down into crevices. Set each piece into a bag, divide remaining salt and spice mixture among the bags (including all that has dropped onto the tray). Add optional ingredients. Close bags, squeezing out as much air as possible, and pack into bowl, cover with plate or pan, and weight. Set in the bottom of the refrigerator, where temperature should remain between 37° and 38°F/3° and 4°C. Within a few hours juices will begin to seep into bag, showing that the curing process is taking place. Turn bags and massage meat daily to be sure salt is penetrating all sides. Curing takes a minimum of 2 weeks, but you

may let meat cure for a month. (If you leave it longer or if bags leak or break, repackage the meat, returning all juices and half again as much new salt to the new bags.)

Preliminary soaking before cooking

Wash off meat in cold water, and soak in a large bowl of cold water, changing it several times—I soak mine for 24 hours to be sure excess salt is out. As the salt leaves the meat, the meat softens and will feel almost like its original self. (Tie with white butcher's twine if you think meat might fall apart during cooking.)

Remarks:

You will note that there is no saltpeter, nitrite, or nitrate in the curing pickle here; thus the cooked meat will be turning a brownish, rather than the storebought reddish, color.

Clockwise: boneless chuck, top round, and fresh pork shoulder

Corned Beef or Pork Boiled Dinner

For 4 to 5 pounds or 2 to 2½ kg meat

1 onion stuck with 4 cloves

1 large carrot

2 celery stalks

A large herb bouquet (8 parsley sprigs, 3 bay leaves, 1 tsp thyme, 3 cloves unpeeled garlic, tied in washed cheesecloth)

Set the meat in a kettle with cold water to cover by 2 inches (5 cm); add the onion, carrot, celery, and herb bouquet. Bring to the simmer, skim off any scum for several minutes, set over it a cover slightly askew for air circulation, and simmer slowly—usually for 3 to 3½ hours, or until meat is tender when pierced with a fork. (Add boiling water if liquid evaporates below level of ingredients; after 2 hours taste meat and add salt to water if needed.)

❶   May be cooked an hour or more in advance and left, partially covered, in its cooking bouillon; reheat slowly before serving.

Serving suggestions

Carve the meat into serving pieces and arrange on a hot platter with, if there is room, the steamed vegetables in the following recipe. Garnish with sprigs of parsley. Moisten with a ladleful of degreased cooking bouillon and pass a pitcher of bouillon, along with the garlic and tomato sauces, for the meat and noodles.

Remarks:

Solid pieces of meat can be carved more attractively than pieces with muscle separations— like those in the beef chuck and in the pork shoulder and the blade end of the pork loin. This is probably why the beef brisket, even though rather stringy in texture, is always popular—it slices evenly; but do note that if you get an edge cut (or double) brisket, you should separate it before carving since you have two muscle layers, each going in a different direction.

A Mixture of Steamed Vegetables

To accompany a boiled dinner and noodles

For 8 people

6 carrots

1 large rutabaga

3 or 4 (or more) white turnips

8 leeks and/or white onions

Enough boiled-dinner bouillon to fill steaming kettle by an inch or so

Fresh parsley

Equipment

A steamer rack or metal colander; a kettle to hold whichever you use; a close-fitting cover

Preliminaries

Since these vegetables all take about the same time to cook, you can arrange them together on the steamer or in the colander; or cook them separately. The number and variety is up to you and the appetites of your guests. To prepare the vegetables, peel the carrots, cut into quarters, and cut the quarters in half. Peel the rutabaga and cut into pieces about the size of the carrots, and do the same with the turnips. Cut the roots off the leeks and cut leeks into 3-inch (8-cm) lengths (saving tender green part of tops for soup); if the leeks show any sign of sand or dirt, split into quarters lengthwise down to within 1 inch (2½ cm) of the root end and wash thoroughly under running water. Drop onions into boiling water, boil 1 minute, then shave off the two ends and slip off the peel; for even, nonburst cooking, pierce a cross ¼ inch (¾ cm) deep in root ends.

❶   Vegetables may be prepared several hours in advance; cover with dampened paper towels and refrigerate in a plastic bag.

Steaming

About half an hour before serving, arrange the vegetables in separate piles on the steamer or in the colander, pour the bouillon into the kettle, and cover closely—if need be, arrange foil over the steamer or colander to make a close seal. Bring to the boil on top of the stove and steam slowly until vegetables are tender; do not overcook—vegetables should just be done.

🕐   If done somewhat ahead, it is best to undercook; set aside partially covered and reheat just before serving.

Serving

Arrange the vegetables either on the platter with the meat or on a separate hot platter; ladle a little of the steaming liquid over them and decorate with parsley sprigs. Add the rest of the savory vegetable steaming liquid to the bouillon you pass with the meat.

Fresh Green Beans Simply Boiled

The fresh green beans here are mostly for color and need no formal recipe since they are so easy to do the French way. Choose crisp snappy ones, rapidly pull off one end, drawing it down the bean to remove any lurking string, and do the same with the other end. Wash in cold water, drain, and, if you are not cooking them soon, wrap in paper towels and refrigerate in a plastic bag. When ready to cook them—which you can do several hours in advance—have a large kettle with 6 quarts or liters rapidly boiling salted water at the ready (for 1 to 2 pounds or ½ to 1 kg beans; you will need the smaller amount for this dinner), drop in the beans, cover the kettle until the beans come back to the boil, then uncover and let beans boil rapidly for 5 minutes or so. Test by eating one or two, and as soon as just cooked through, set a metal colander curved side down in the kettle and tip to drain the beans. Then, with colander still in, refresh the beans for several minutes in cold water—you can even add ice cubes to the water to speed the cooling. This sets the fresh green color and the texture.

🕐   If boiled in advance, drain thoroughly and refrigerate in a clean towel.

Shortly before serving, toss in a large frying pan for a moment to evaporate excess moisture, then toss with butter, drops of lemon juice, and salt and pepper to taste. Or drop for a minute or so in a kettle of boiling salted water, drain, and serve at once. (Or serve cold, with oil and lemon dressing, a sprinkling of minced shallots or scallions, and parsley.)

Cream of Garlic Sauce with Horseradish

To serve with boiled dinners, boiled fish or chicken, boiled potatoes

For about 2 cups or ½ liter

1 large head garlic
2 Tb butter
½ cup (1 dL) dry white French vermouth
1 Tb cornstarch
2 cups (½ L) bouillon from the boiled dinner, or from another source
1 or more Tb white prepared horseradish
1 egg yolk
4 Tb heavy cream (a little more if you wish)
Salt and white pepper
2 Tb fresh minced herbs, such as parsley and chives

To peel the garlic cloves, separate them from the head and drop into boiling water for 1 minute; the skins will slip off easily. Then simmer with the butter in a small saucepan for 5 minutes without browning; add the vermouth, cover, and simmer 10 to 15 minutes more or until very tender and liquid has evaporated completely. Purée by rubbing through a sieve with a wooden spoon, then scrape garlic off sieve back into saucepan. Blend in the cornstarch, gradually beat in the bouillon, and bring to the simmer, stirring. Simmer 2 minutes and remove from heat. In a small bowl, blend 1 tablespoon horseradish, the egg yolk, and 4 tablespoons cream; by dribbles beat in half of the hot sauce, then by dribbles beat this mixture back into the pan with the rest of the sauce. Bring again to the simmer, stirring, and taste carefully for seasoning, adding salt and pepper and more horseradish and cream if you wish.

◑   May be prepared in advance. Set aside off heat, and float a spoonful of cream over surface of sauce to prevent a skin from forming.

Reheat just before serving, stir in the herbs, and pour into a warm sauce bowl.

Fresh Tomato Fondue

A sauce to serve with boiled meats—or with fish, eggs, soufflés, and so forth

For about 2 cups or ½ liter

8 to 10 firm ripe red tomatoes—plus some drained and strained Italian plum tomatoes for added taste and color if you feel them needed

2 Tb olive oil

2 Tb minced shallots or scallions

1 clove minced garlic (optional)

¼ tsp thyme

1 bay leaf

Salt and pepper

Peel, seed, and juice the tomatoes, and dice them into pieces of about ⅜ inch (1 cm). Heat the oil in a medium-size saucepan, stir in the shallots or scallions and optional garlic, simmer a moment, then add the tomato (and strained canned tomato if you are using it). Add the thyme and bay leaf and simmer several minutes, tossing and folding, until tomatoes have rendered their excess juice and have formed a fairly thick sauce. Season carefully with salt and pepper. Serve hot, warm, or cold—without the bay leaf.

🕐   May be cooked in advance.

Homemade Noodles

Kneaded and cut in a noodle machine

For about 24 ounces (675 g) noodles, or the equivalent of 2 standard boxes of commercial egg noodles, serving 8 people generously

The Noodle Dough:

1 ¾ cups (4 dL) all-purpose flour

2 "large" eggs

2 to 4 Tb cold water

Equipment

A mixing bowl, wooden spoon, and rubber spatula, or a food processor; a noodle machine (either hand-crank or electric); 1 or 2 clean broom handles to be suspended (for instance, between 2 chairs)

Forming the noodle dough by hand
Place the flour in a mixing bowl, make a well in the center, and break in the 2 eggs; blend them with 2 tablespoons of the water, and gradually mix in the surrounding flour with a wooden spoon or a spatula. Blend vigorously to make a stiff dough; turn out onto a work surface and knead vigorously with the heel of your hand, adding droplets more water to unblended bits. Dough should just form into a mass—the machine will do the rest.

For the food processor

Add all ingredients to the machine, using 2 tablespoons water, and process (using metal cutting blade); in about a minute, if you have enough water for the temper of the day, the dough will usually form itself into a ball on top of the blade. Sometimes the dough will not form a mass but seem to be made up of granular particles; however, as long as you can squeeze it into a coherent mass when removed from the food processor, all is well. In any case, experience will be your judge as to whether or not to add droplets more water. Turn dough out onto work surface and knead together to blend. Dough should be firm; if soft and/or sticky, knead in a sprinkling of flour.

Remarks:

A little too much water, in my book, is no disaster, since you can always knead in more flour to make the requisitely stiff dough. Again, your own experience will guide you, eventually, but don't be afraid of the dough. Not much can go wrong as long as it is stiff enough and dry enough to pass through the kneading and cutting rollers of your machine. Tenderness and exquisiteness of texture can come later, and will be part of your own particular secret genius with the noodle.

🕐 Dough may be formed half an hour or so in advance, and some practitioners prefer to let the dough rest before forming it; in this case, wrap it airtight in plastic to keep it from crusting over. (I have found, by the way, that dough made with unbleached flour turns a grayish yellow when refrigerated overnight; however,

it kneads and cooks up satisfactorily when cooked the next day.) Freshly made dough may be frozen.

Finishing the dough and forming noodles

Cut the dough in half and cover one piece with plastic while forming the other. Flatten this piece of dough into a cake the size of your palm, and pinch one edge so it will fit into the machine. Set smooth rollers to their widest opening—number 8 on most machines. Crank the dough through. Fold dough in half, end to end, and crank through several times until dough is smooth and fairly evenly rectangular; as necessary, brush dough with flour before passing through rollers, since it will stick to the machine if it is too damp.

When dough is smooth, reset rollers to the next-lower setting and crank it through, then to the next lower, and the next—which is usually number 5. By this time your strip of dough will be so long you will probably want to cut it in two; now pass the first and then the second half through number 4, the setting that gives, I think, the right thinness for noodles and lasagne. Hang each strip as it is finished on a broom handle to dry out briefly (but not to stiffen—4 to 5 minutes are usually enough). Repeat the process with the reserved piece of dough, then crank the dried strips through the noodle roller, set at number 4, and hang noodles on broom handles as you cut them.

🕐 Noodles may be formed and cooked at once, or formed in advance and cooked later. For instance, you may let them hang on the broom handles until they have dried thoroughly, and then package them. Or you

may like to preserve them in a semifresh state. In this case, arrange a layer of noodles on a tray, sprinkle corn flour over lightly (if you can't find corn flour, pulverize cornmeal in your blender), cover with wax paper, and continue with successive layers of noodles, ending with wax paper; set in the refrigerator overnight, or until dry, then package in their laid-out state, and freeze. (If you freeze noodles when they are damp they will stick together, and it is almost impossible to separate the strands while they cook.)

Cooking Noodles:

A large kettle filled with at least 8 quarts or liters rapidly boiling water

2 tsp salt per quart of water

A large colander (for draining)

Butter and olive oil (or your choice of dressing)

A hot platter and 2 large forks for tossing and serving

Salt and pepper

About 5 minutes before serving, plunge the noodles into the rapidly boiling water and cover until boil is reached. Then boil uncovered, frequently testing the noodle cooking by eating a strand or two—fresh soft noodles take but a minute of cooking, while semifresh and dry noodles take a minute or two longer. Do not overcook or the noodles will be mushy— better slightly under- than slightly overcooked.

Once they are done, drain in a colander, shaking vigorously to remove excess water. Spread a little butter and oil (or dressing) in the platter, turn into it the steaming noodles, and toss with the forks, adding salt and pepper, more butter and oil (or dressing), and tasting to be sure all is perfectly seasoned. Work rapidly and rush them to the table, still steaming.

Strawberries en Chemise

Icing-coated strawberries, to decorate desserts and ice cream

---

For 24 large strawberries

---

1 cup sifted confectioners sugar (a little more if needed)

1 tsp raw egg white (a little more if needed)

¼ tsp fresh lemon juice

Drops of Cognac or more lemon juice (as needed)

Fresh strawberries, washed rapidly and laid on a rack

Equipment

A portable electric mixer or a wire whip

Place the sugar, egg white, and lemon juice in a smallish high-sided mixing bowl and beat a minute or more with electric mixer or wire whip until sugar forms a quite stiff mass that "forms the beak"—makes stiff points when a bit is lifted in the blades of the beater. Thin out with a droplet or two of Cognac or more lemon juice—icing should be thick enough to enrobe strawberries. Holding a berry by its topknot, swirl it in the frosting to cover two-thirds the way up its sides, and replace on rack.

🕐   May be done an hour in advance.

Arrange over strawberry sherbet or ice cream just before bringing to the table.

⏲ *Timing*

Boiling and draining the noodles is *the* last-minute job for this dinner. They must be eaten the moment they're done, and homemade ones take only minutes to cook. About 20 minutes before putting on the water for the noodles, start the vegetables steaming. *N.B.:* If you plan to add the optional green beans to the vegetable bouquet, blanch them and refrigerate that afternoon, and toss in butter right after you've put the noodles into the pot.

The two sauces are quick to make, and the strawberries, to dip. But remember to put the sherbet or ice cream in the refrigerator to soften at about the time you sit down to dinner.

You should start cooking the corned meat about 3½ hours before you eat it, and it must be soaked for 24 hours before that. Salt and spice it at least 2 weeks in advance, though it can stay in its brine for 2 months. And don't forget to massage and turn it every day during that 2-week period.

One nice thing about shopping for this dinner is that every ingredient except the strawberries (and, if you're having them, the green beans) can be bought days in advance.

Pasta primavera—cooked noodles have been tossed in slivered garlic and oil, then simmered in heavy cream (or béchamel); now blanched, diced, buttered fresh vegetables are added; and finally cheese is sprinkled over all.

Menu Variations

The main course: Rather than cured meat, you may like fresh meat with noodles, or a boiled fowl; if you do either, I'd suggest adding a cooking sausage, such as chorizo or Polish kielbasy. Salted goose or duck would be elegant and is made in exactly the same way as corned meat. Both are simple cousins of the French preserve, or *confit.*

Noodles are delicious tossed in olive oil in which you have sautéed a clove of garlic; they are then simmered in cream and tossed with cheese. You could elaborate on this, especially in summer, by adding a bouquet of bright diced and cooked vegetables and tossing again for a Pasta alla Primavera. Going further, you could add diced ham.

The pasta machine Paul and I have makes either thin or medium-width noodles; and, as you know, noodle dough tastes quite different in its many forms. A lasagna made with uncut homemade noodle dough is an experience (for a nice recipe, see the French-Italian one in *J.C.'s Kitchen*). Most general cookbooks—and most ethnic ones, for that matter—have useful suggestions for other, myriad uses of this dough.

The dessert: I do think something light and fruit flavored will taste best to you after noodles and cured meat: a homemade sherbet, perhaps (see "VIP Lunch," page 49), or a fruit compote. Or you could offer a basket of fresh fruit. The children will enjoy arranging a lovely still life and maybe learn to eat even such difficult delights as ripe figs in the French manner, with knife and fork.

Leftovers

You can rinse leftover cooked *pasta* by a quick plunge in boiling water; then drain well and serve hot with any of an enormous variety of accompaniments. Or use it, rinsed in cold water after draining and drained again, in a composed salad. Leftover raw pasta can be frozen.

Cured meat can be reheated, even several times. Sliced, it makes splendid sandwiches, or can be served as a salad platter. Ground and mixed with chard, cheese, and egg (see *Mastering II*), it makes a fine hamburger. I'd add sausage meat if I planned a meat loaf or patties. You can make a vegetable-and-meat loaf, to serve with tomato sauce, as follows: run leftover vegetables, along with noodles, through the food processor; then process twice as much meat. Combine these ingredients, then add 1 egg for each 2 cups (½ L) of the mixture, add a bit of sausage meat for richness, mix, and bake. To make that delicious classic, corned beef hash—or for that matter, corned pork hash—see page 12. Also, if you have boned your own pork loin for corning, you'll find you have enough pork meat clinging to the bone to make scrapple, page 14.

The bouillon is delicious; why not add to it some of the leftover noodles, some of the meat, and some of the vegetables for a splendid soup? A bit of the *garlic sauce* would be excellent with either this soup or the meat loaf.

Postscript: On cooking with children

Influenced, perhaps, by my early experience at a Montessori school, and surely by living in a clan full of carvers, painters, carpenters, and cooks of all ages, I am all for encouraging children to work productively with their hands. They learn to handle and care for equipment with respect. It is good to give them knives, for instance, as early as you dare. A knife is a tool, not a toy. A sharp, clean knife is safer to use than a dull, rusty one—easier too: a four-year-old will discover that for himself as you teach him to slice a hard-boiled egg neatly and then to fillet a fish. Talk to children as you plan menus. Let their small, sensitive noses sniff the fish as you shop. Work together at the counter and let your children arrange platters. Nothing gives them more pleasure than setting things in rows and rosettes.

The small rituals, like the clean hands and clean apron before setting to work; the precision of gesture, like leveling off a cupful of flour; the charm of improvisation and making something new; the pride of mastery; and the gratification of offering something one has made—these have such value to a child. And where are they so easily to be obtained as in cooking? The patience and good humor demanded of you by cooking with a child are a good investment.

Do taste everything together, at every stage, and serve to children what you eat yourself. Once they have enough teeth to cope with any food, children, with their unjaded palates, are a keen, responsive audience for an enthusiastic cook.

A French classic, with a great California salad.

Soup for Supper

Menu
For 6 people

*French Onion Soup Gratinée — With bowls of
grated cheese and a large basket of
toasted French bread rounds*

❧

*Cobb Salad — A mixture of fresh greens with
Roquefort cheese, avocado, eggs, herbs,
chicken, and other delicacies*

❧

Vesuvial Bananas — A flambéed extravaganza

❧

*Suggested wines:
A moderately hearty red wine, like a
Beaujolais or zinfandel; and a sweet wine,
sparkling wine, or Champagne with
the dessert*

It could be said that the onion has done a lot
more for France than Napoleon, and deserves
its own Arch of Triumph, whose design might
include bas-reliefs of grateful peasants holding
soup tureens over their hearts, in salute to onion soup and the comfort and sense of luxury
that it has brought over centuries to France's
thrifty farmers. All it takes is onions from the
kitchen garden, broth from Sunday's boiled
dinner (maybe the week's only meat, so its
juices provide a welcome memory), cheese and
wine very likely made at home, and yesterday's
hard bread: not a crumb wasted, and its stale-
ness treated as a virtue. So far as I know, the
French haven't built it a monument, but they
do honor their national dish by calling it *soupe
à l'oignon,* in the singular not the plural;
otherwise they say *soupe aux pois, aux ca-
rottes,* etc.: not onions, in other words, but
The Onion.

No other soup can compare in flavor
with the rich, mahogany-colored brew of
slowly caramelized onions simmered in a
meaty broth; and it can be expanded into a
hearty one-dish meal, La Gratinée Lyonnaise,
by alternately layering the tureen with toasted
rounds of French bread and cheese, right up to
the top, pouring in soup to fill every cranny,
and slowly baking to produce a fragrant onion
and cheese pudding. This is described farther
on as a variation of the classic recipe, along
with other ways of using this excellent soup.

It's excellent at any time of day, too. In
our youthful Paris years, we had it to top off a
night on the town at one of the all-night cafés
in Les Halles, the central market that no longer
exists. At the same time, onion soup was eaten
for breakfast by the farmers who'd just carted
in their produce and by the *titis parisiens* and

the *forts des Halles*, the blue-smocked work-men and porters, who took their soup with a *p'tit coup* of red wine and a *p'tit coup de fouet*, a whiplash of bitter coffee: guaranteed to grow hair on the chest—or depilate it, I suspect, if applied externally. On cold evenings nowadays when we come home in need of a quick restorative, we've even been known to heat up canned onion soup, pour a bit of wine into it, slice and toast some of the homemade French bread we frequently have on hand, and float it on the soup with plenty of grated cheese from the freezer. And it makes a fine lunch for unexpected guests: a meal in itself if you wind it up with a basket of crisp, chilled apples. We find both canned and dehydrated onion soup extremely good; homemade is just that much better, simply because it tastes homemade. (A warning, however: you don't gain anything by slicing and cooking your own onions if you then simmer them in canned broth—the result will taste as though all of it came out of a can.)

Homemade stock couldn't be easier. Plan to make it some day when you'll be at home, starting it after breakfast and letting it simmer practically unattended until dinnertime. Its presence in the freezer makes homemade onion soup an easy possibility when you're planning a company menu. For anything but a formal dinner, a hearty soup can certainly be the centerpiece of a meal, and you can't beat onion for popularity, especially when you dress it up with Cognac and top it with a beautiful gratin of mixed cheeses. Then, for more drama at the table, just before serving tweak up a corner of the puffy, bubbling, fragrant gratin and stir in egg yolks whisked with Port wine. It imparts a smooth texture, the flavor booms out like a gong, and there's something warm and hospitable about this final gesture. When our nieces and nephews were

little, we'd sometimes give them purses or wallets for Christmas, and Paul always slipped in a shiny dime before wrapping them; the feeling is a bit like that.

If it's an informal supper party, you might well prefer the statelier pace, and of course the variety, of a three-course menu, simple though it may be, with a pretty, light dessert and a fairly substantial salad. The one I am suggesting here was born in California, certainly the cradle of salads in this country. I am not, by the way, offering anything like the one I shall always remember at a ladies' luncheon (of non-Californians) some years ago; it was composed of chopped marshmallows and bottled mayonnaise molded with pineapple gelatin into the shape of a peeled banana and posed upright on one piece of pale iceberg lettuce far too small for the cleverest of diners to hide anything under. No. I am proposing a famous salad served for the first time at the Hollywood Brown Derby, not the original restaurant designed by Wilson Mizener in the shape of a hat on Wilshire Boulevard, but the Brown Derby at Hollywood and Vine.

It was invented there in 1936 by Robert Cobb, president of the restaurant group, who apparently improvised the dish from leftovers

The original Brown Derby Restaurant, Wilshire Boulevard, Los Angeles

in the refrigerator, just as any cook will serve a few savory scraps on lettuce and call it a chef's salad. But Cobb's leftovers included good Roquefort cheese, chicken, avocado, bacon, hard-boiled eggs, herbs, tomatoes, and a variety of salad greens; he diced them fine, the greens too, and tossed them all together. An epicure's inspiration. He was bragging about his invention one day when Syd Grauman came to the restaurant. Grauman wanted one, and he found it so good he told all his friends about Cobb's marvelous salad. Friends told friends, and so forth . . . And no wonder. Each mouthful rewards you with a whole spectrum of delicious flavors, and of textures ranging from rich and suave to downright crunchy.

You present Cobb Salad beautifully arranged in strips or segments, and then you have the fun of tossing it into confetti, a savage joy rather like jumbling up a completed jigsaw puzzle before passing it on to your little brother. A more sophisticated pleasure, if you enjoy tabletop cookery, is the concoction of Vesuvial Bananas in a chafing dish. It takes a good 5 minutes for the sauce to boil down to a syrup while the bananas cook through, and when I'm all alone on the stage or the TV screen, I have to have some trifle ready to fill the silence like "Life in California in the Golden Age of Cobb (or of Caesar, he of that other salad)" or even "Big Bananas I Have Known." But at home, you don't need talk or stunts. The bananas are spectacle enough, from the appetizing sizzles of their buttery beginning, through the expanding fragrances of their liquorous cooking, right on to the climactic fiery cloudlet of their final moment. Certainly, good points about this menu are its relative ease of preparation and its quite reasonable expense—take or leave a few dollops of wine and spirits along the way—and, except for a rapid change of plates between courses, you can be in the dining room with your guests the whole way through.

Preparations and Marketing

Recommended Equipment:
To serve the soup, you'll need either a 3-quart (3-L) ovenproof tureen, or else individual ovenproof bowls. For slicing onions, you can use (in order of expense and splendor): a sharp knife; an efficient small slicer, The Feemster, made by the M. E. Heuk Company, Cincinnati, Ohio 45223; a cabbage shredder often shown in country store catalogues; the chic and intricate *mandoline* manufactured in France by the Bron people (and maybe other companies); or a food processor.

To serve Cobb Salad, a wide bowl is desirable, so that you can present it, before tossing, with each colorful ingredient mounded separately on the greens.

Although you can do the Vesuvial Bananas in an electric skillet at the table, a chafing dish setup is far more attractive. You do not need the intense heat provided by the fluid-alcohol flame in our professional burner (page 106), but it must be strong enough to cook the orange syrup in a reasonable amount of time. In my numerous struggles with public flaming, I've found it perfectly satisfactory to take a can of Sterno and either remove the lid and use the can itself as a container, or scoop the material into a small metal bowl with a top diameter of about 4 inches (10 cm). What you need is a large burning surface that you can rig to fit your chafing dish contraption. I also find it a good idea to set the chafing dish apparatus on a tray to catch spills, hold utensils, etc.

Staples to Have on Hand:

Table salt
Optional: coarse or kosher salt
Peppercorns
Sugar
Imported bay leaves
Dried thyme
Whole cloves or allspice berries
Olive oil and/or fresh peanut oil
Flour
Eggs (3 to 5)
Unsalted butter (less than 2 sticks)
Garlic
Optional: Port or Madeira wine

Orange liqueur
White rum, dark Jamaica rum, or bourbon
    whiskey
Optional: Cognac

Specific Ingredients for This Menu:

Meaty soup bones (2 or more quarts, or 2 L;
    see recipe, plus suggestions for a boiled
    dinner in Manufacturing Note preceding
    recipe)
Boneless chicken breast halves (2)
Bacon (6 slices)

Roquefort or best-quality blue cheese (2 ounces
or 60 g)

Firm Swiss cheese, of several kinds, if possible—
such as Gruyère, Emmenthal, Fribourg,
Sbrinz (9 ounces or 250 g)

Salad greens: 1 green crisp head iceberg lettuce;
1 smallish head chicory; 1 smallish head
romaine; 1 medium-to-large bunch
watercress ▼

Parsley ▼

Shallots ▼, scallions, or chives

Celery (1 head)

Optional: 1 leek

Yellow onions (about 3½ pounds or 1½ kg)

Carrots (2 large)

Tomatoes (2; see Cobb Salad recipe)

Avocado (1)

Lemons (2)

Oranges (2)

Bananas (6) ▼

An accompaniment for the bananas: fresh
strawberries (2 pints or 900 g)

Dry white wine or dry white French vermouth
(2½ cups or about ½ L)

Bread for French Onion Soup ▼

▶ **Remarks:**

Salad greens: surround with slightly dampened paper towels, and store in plastic bags
in the refrigerator. Wash watercress, shake or
spin fairly dry, wrap in paper towels, and
refrigerate in a plastic bag—cress is perish-
able and will keep only about 2 days before
beginning to turn yellow. *Parsley* is more
sturdy: prepare like watercress, but it will
keep several days longer. *Shallots:* shallots
will keep in a cool, dry place for a number
of weeks, but if you happen to have more
than you need, you can freeze them whole, in
a plastic bag or container. They soften up as
soon as they thaw, so peel and mince them
almost as soon as you take them from the

freezer; they are then fine for cooking,
though too limp for salads. *Bananas:* for
cooking, they should be just barely ripe—all
yellow, but without any soft spots. Store at
room temperature. *Bread for French onion
soup:* you want white bread with body here;
if it is soft and fluffy and squashy to begin
with, it will become a miserable disintegra-
tion of white slime when baked in the soup.
Ideally you would use old-fashioned French
bread, from the regular long loaf cut into
crosswise slices less than ½ inch (1 cm)
thick. But if your French bread is soft and
limp, you will be better off with a firm loaf
of nonsweet sliced sandwich bread, cut into
rounds about 3 inches (7 to 8 cm) in diameter.
If you have any doubts, toast a slice of bread
and simmer it to see what happens. Your
own homemade French bread would, of
course, be ideal.

The right kind—and the wrong kind—of French bread

French Onion Soup

Entirely homemade onion soup base

Manufacturing Note:
As long as you are making a beef stock, you may also want to include the ingredients for a boiled dinner, such as a piece of stewing beef or pork, or a chicken, or a fresh beef tongue. Tie it up and attach a long end of its string to the handle of your kettle; then you can pull it up for checking, and remove it when it's done. If you want vegetables with this boiled dinner, tie them in a piece of washed cheesecloth, and they are easy to remove, too, when their time is up.

**Plain Brown Beef Stock —
Fonds Brun Simple:**
*For about 2 quarts or 2 L,
serving 4 to 6 people*

For the Beef Stock:

2 or more quarts (2 L) sawed beef bones, including knuckles and some meaty scraps attached; plus veal and poultry bones, raw and/or cooked

2 large carrots, scrubbed and roughly sliced

3 large onions, peeled and roughly chopped

Sufficient cold water to cover all ingredients

1 large leek, washed (optional)

3 celery ribs with leaves, washed

1 Tb coarse or kosher salt (or table salt)

1 large herb bouquet tied in washed cheesecloth (8 parsley sprigs, 1 large imported bay leaf, 1 tsp dried thyme, 4 whole cloves or allspice berries, 3 large cloves garlic, unpeeled)

Spread the bones and meat scraps (except for poultry) and the carrots and onions in a roomy enough roasting pan; set in the upper middle level of a 450°F/230°C oven and roast for 40 or more minutes, turning and basting ingredients several times with accumulated fat until nicely browned. Transfer to a large soup kettle, leaving fat in pan. Discard fat and deglaze pan—pour in a cup or so (¼ L) of water and set over heat, scraping coagulated roasting juices into the liquid. Pour into the kettle, and add enough cold water to cover ingredients by 2 inches (5 cm). Bring to the simmer, skim off gray scum that will rise to the surface for several minutes, then add rest of ingredients. Cover partially and simmer slowly 4 to 5 hours at least, adding more water if needed to cover ingredients. Strain into a large bowl, chill, peel coagulated fat off surface, and your stock is finished.

Before and after—browned bones and vegetables at top

⦿ Stock may be refrigerated in a covered bowl, but needs boiling up every 2 or 3 days to prevent spoilage; or it may be frozen for several months. If your stock lacks savor, boil it down in a large kettle (after degreasing) to concentrate it.

Meat Glaze—Glace de Viande:

You can concentrate your stock even further, almost to the consistency of a bouillon cube, actually. Keep on boiling it down until the stock thickens into a syrup (be careful near the end since it burns easily); pour into a jar, and cover it. Meat glaze will keep for months in the refrigerator, ready at all times to enrich a soup or a sauce, or to become a bouillon. A real kitchen treasure to have on hand, and it doesn't take up much space, either.

For the Onion Soup:

3 Tb butter

1 Tb olive oil or cooking oil

6 cups (1 ½ L) quite thinly sliced yellow onions (about 1 ½ pounds or ¾ kg)

½ tsp sugar (which helps the onions to brown)

1 tsp salt

Six cups of onions cook down to less than one when really caramelized.

2 Tb flour

2 quarts (2 L) homemade stock, heated (the preceding recipe)

2 cups (½ L) dry white wine or dry white French vermouth

Salt and pepper as needed

Melt the butter with the oil in a heavy-bottomed 4-quart (3 ¾-L) pan; stir in the sliced onions. Cover the pan and cook slowly for 15 to 20 minutes (or cook them in a 350°F/180°C oven), stirring up occasionally, until onions are tender and translucent. Raise heat to moderately high, stir in the sugar and salt, and cook 20 to 30 minutes more, stirring frequently, until onions have turned a fine deep caramel brown.

Lower heat to moderate, blend in the flour, and cook, stirring, for 2 to 3 minutes. Remove from heat, and blend in 2 ladlefuls hot stock. Stir in the rest, and the wine. Season lightly to taste, bring to the boil, then simmer slowly, partially covered, for 30 minutes. Carefully correct seasoning.

⦿ May be cooked several days in advance. When cold, cover and refrigerate, or freeze.

Serve as is, with a bowl of grated cheese and toasted French bread, or make onion soup gratinée as follows:

French Onion Soup Gratinée— The Classic Version

There are a number of opinions on the very best recipe for gratinéed onion soup. My French colleague Simca has her excellent version in Volume I of *Mastering*, and I did it also for *The French Chef* black-and-white TV series: it has a little grated raw onion and some slivers of cheese in the soup before its toast and cheese topping go on, and it finishes with a *de luxe* enrichment of Worcestershire sauce, egg yolk, and Cognac that is slipped under the brown crust just before serving. A trip through other French sources confirms a spirited egg-yolk finish, and also reveals conflicting information on what can cut down on the length of the cheese strings that drip from the spoon as you consume your soup—although certainly to some enthusiasts those dangling ropes of cheese are a large part of the soup's authentic character.

Stringy cheese solutions
1) Rather than grating the cheese, either cut it into small dice or very thin slices. 2) Use two or three kinds of cheese rather than just one. 3) Beat egg yolks into the soup before gratinéing, and bake it in a pan of boiling water. 4) White wine can de-string cheese—as suggested by Jim Beard and confirmed by the French—and it does indeed work for a cheese sauce. Well, I've tried all but method number 3, and my soup-cheese does string somewhat, though not excessively. However, I think one should select pieces of cheese that are on the rather hard and dry side, and I do use a good bit of spirits.

For a 3-quart or 3-L ovenproof tureen or casserole, serving 4 to 6 people

A loaf or 2 of firm, full-textured French bread
2 Tb or more butter
3 ounces (85 g) firm Swiss cheese in a piece, cut into very thin slices
Freshly ground pepper—2 to 3 turns of the pepper mill
2 quarts (2 L) or so simmering onion soup
4 to 5 Tb Cognac (optional)
1 ¼ cups (3 dL) lightly packed, coarsely grated mixed Swiss cheeses
2 egg yolks, beaten with 4 to 5 Tb Port or Madeira wine (optional)

Equipment:

An ovenproof tureen or casserole; a serving spoon and fork for the crust; a ladle for serving the soup; and a platter on which to set the tureen. A small decorative pitcher for the optional egg yolk and wine mixture

Toasted French Bread Rounds:

Preheat oven to 425°F/220°C. Cut bread into slices less than ½ inch (1 cm) thick, place in one layer on a baking sheet or sheets, and dry out in upper third (or middle and upper third) level of oven, watching and turning frequently until bread is a fairly even lightly toasted brown. (You may want extra bread rounds to pass with the soup; do them now, too, and/or do extras, since they freeze nicely for several weeks.)

Filling and baking the tureen
About 45 minutes

Preheat oven to 425°F/220°C. Smear a tablespoon of butter in bottom of tureen and arrange over it a closely packed layer of toasted bread; spread over bread layer the sliced cheese, grind on pepper, ladle in the boiling soup, and pour in the optional Cognac. Float a closely packed layer of toast on the top of the soup, and spread over it the grated cheese with a few grinds of pepper; sprinkle over that a tablespoon or 2 melted butter. Set tureen in middle level of oven and bake for about half an hour, or until soup is bubbling hot and top has browned nicely.

🕐 Plan to serve the soup fairly soon, for fear the crust might sink down into it. Until then, keep it hot, almost at the simmer.

At the table, and just before serving, lift a side of the crust with a serving fork, pour into the soup the optional egg yolk–wine mixture, and stir gently under crust with your ladle. Serve, giving each guest some of the top crust along with the soup.

Individual Servings of French Onion Soup Gratinée:

Use the same system as that outlined above, but make individual servings in ovenproof earthenware bowls set on a sturdy baking sheet; they will take about 20 minutes in the oven.

Adding spirited finish to onion soup at the table

Preparing an individual bowl of onion soup

**Thick French Onion Soup—
La Gratinée Lyonnaise:**

Proceed in exactly the same way as in the
master recipe, but fill the tureen with layer
upon layer of toasted bread rounds, each
topped with a mixture of grated cheese and
sliced cheese. (You will need probably 1½
times more cheese and soup than the
amounts specified.) Pour the soup in to cover
the bread and bake for 30 minutes or until
soup is absorbed and cheese has browned on
top; then pour in more soup and bake another 5 to 10 minutes. Stir in the optional
egg yolk and wine mixture at the table. The
bread and soup will have combined and
transformed themselves into a richly flavored,
soft, melting cheese and onion dumpling in
your bowl—a very special Old World dish.

Cobb Salad

Ingredients for 6 to 8 people

½ head firm fine green iceberg lettuce

1 small head chicory (frizzy lettuce)

½ medium head romaine

1 medium bunch watercress—to make a cup
or so (¼ L) of leaves and tender stems

2 poached chicken breast halves (see
directions at end of this recipe)

Salt

Freshly ground pepper

1 lemon

Olive oil or fresh peanut oil

6 slices crisply cooked bacon

3 hard-boiled eggs

2 Tb minced fresh chives (or the white part
and some of the tender green of scallions, or
a mixture of shallots and fresh parsley)

2 ounces (60 g) real Roquefort cheese or
best-quality blue cheese

2 medium-sized ripe red firm tomatoes (out
of season, mix tomatoes with drained,
seeded, Italian plum tomatoes and/or canned
red pimiento)

*The gratinée has numerous layers of
bread and cheese.*

**About 1 cup (¼ L) plain vinaigrette dressing
(page 110)**

1 fine ripe firm avocado

🕐 **Preliminaries**
*(To be done several hours in advance if
necessary)*

Separate the leaves of the salad greens, discard tough or wilted parts, wash leaves and
spin dry; wrap loosely and refrigerate in a
clean towel. Pull off leaves and tender stems
from watercress (discard tough bits); wash,
wrap in a damp paper towel, and refrigerate
in a plastic bag. Cut the chicken breasts into
fine dice (by first cutting into thin slices, the
slices into strips, and the strips laid lengthwise, then cut crosswise into dice, as illustrated); toss in a small bowl with a sprinkling
of salt and pepper, a few drops of
lemon juice and of oil; cover and refrigerate.
Mince the cooked bacon and set aside in
another bowl; chop or sieve the eggs (or use
the 3-way egg-slicer method illustrated), and
toss in another small bowl with a sprinkling
of salt and pepper. Mince the chives or scallions fine, and put them in the bowl with the
eggs, and do the same with the Roquefort
or blue cheese (dicing in the same fashion as

you did either the chicken or the eggs; you
should have about ½ cup or 1 dL diced). Drop
the tomatoes for exactly 10 seconds in boiling
water, and set aside (to loosen their skins for
later peeling). Prepare the vinaigrette.

🕐 **Half an hour or so before serving**
(Items that wilt if done too soon)

Choose a fine big salad bowl. With a large,
very sharp knife, cut the salad greens into
very fine dice, ³/₁₆ inch or ½ cm. The easiest
method, I think, is to lay 3 or 4 leaves flat,
cut them into fine julienne shreds, pile the
shreds together lengthwise, and cut across
them—as for the chicken. The object here is
to make clean nonbruising cuts. Place the
greens in the bowl, mince the watercress
also, and add to the greens. Peel, seed, and
juice the tomatoes (cut out stem, peel, halve
horizontally—not through stem— squeeze
each half gently and poke out seeds, as illustrated); dice fine, and set aside on your chopping board with a sprinkling of salt and
pepper. Halve the avocado (as illustrated);
peel and dice it, and scoop into a sieve, then
swish in a bowl of cold water for a moment
and drain (water bath helps prevent avocado
from discoloring); turn into a small bowl and

*Chicken breasts are first cut into strips,
then diced.*

Egg slicer makes HB eggs easy to dice.

*Blanching has loosened the tomato
skin, for peeling.*

*A gentle squeeze ejects tomato seeds
and juice.*

*Open the cut avocado with a twist of
the wrist.*

fold with a sprinkling of salt and a few drops of lemon juice and of oil.

🕐 **Just before serving**

Beat up the vinaigrette and toss about ⅓ of it with the minced greens, taste for seasoning, adding a little more dressing, salt, and pepper, etc., if necessary; arrange greens in a shallow mound. Arrange the rest of the ingredients attractively over the greens. Present at once to the table for general admiration, then toss the salad and serve it forth.

Note: If you wish to arrange the salad somewhat in advance, do not season the various ingredients, or they will lose their freshness; arrange the salad, cover with plastic and refrigerate, then toss with the dressing at the table.

Variations:

Arrange the salad in individual bowls, and each guest may then toss his own — or not — as he desires. You may substitute fresh mushrooms for chicken, or shrimp, crab, ham, or lobster; capers are also permitted when accompanying anchovies.

Poached Chicken Breasts:

Lay boned chicken breast halves in a lightly buttered saucepan just large enough to hold them in one layer. Pour in ½ cup (1 dL) dry white wine or dry white French vermouth, enough cold water just to cover the breasts, and add a bay leaf, a finely minced shallot or scallion, 3 parsley sprigs, 4 peppercorns, and ½ teaspoon of salt. Bring just to the simmer, cover, and cook at the barest simmer for 8 to 10 minutes, until the meat is springy to the touch. Let cool for 30 minutes in the cooking broth, then drain, let cool, wrap, and refrigerate. (Save cooking broth and add to your store of chicken stock, or use in soups and sauces.)

Vesuvial Bananas

Bananas simmered in orange butter and flamed in rum

Almost everyone loves bananas, and they make a most delectable flaming dessert when you want a chafing dish finish. Desserts done at the table demand the drama of flaming and, besides, that burning evaporates the alcohol — what we want with our bananas is the flavor of those spirits, not the kick! Although you may serve them just as they are, I think you'll find they most definitely need something to dress them up, such as a mound of sherbet or ice cream that they might surround, or a sprinkling of cinnamon or shaved chocolate. My solution is strawberries sliced and spread over

Professionals use this alcohol-fueled burner for tabletop cookery.

the banana midriffs and placed whole at their
either ends, then a basting of all elements with
the buttery cooking juices.

For 6 people

Note: Because of timing restrictions on
our television program, I did only 4
bananas, but our dinner here is for 6
people and so is the following recipe.

2 oranges
½ cup (1 dL) sugar
¾ stick (3 ounces or 85 g) unsalted butter
5 Tb orange liqueur
5 Tb white rum, dark Jamaica rum, or bourbon whiskey
1 lemon
1 pint (½ L) fresh strawberries, halved or quartered lengthwise
1 pint (½ L) fresh strawberries, whole, stems removed
6 bananas

Equipment:
A chafing dish large enough to hold the bananas easily; a burner with a reasonably strong heat source (or an electric frying pan); a tray to set the cooking apparatus upon; a long-handled spoon and fork for the bananas; a table fork for the lemon; a platter and/or dessert plates

Preliminaries in the kitchen

Arrange the dining room accessories on the
tray. Just before dinner, so it will not lose its
freshness, grate the peel of 1 orange onto a
decorative plate, with the sugar and butter.
Squeeze the juice out of 1½ of the oranges and
pour into a pitcher; refrigerate, along with the
butter and sugar plate. Set out the bottles of
orange liqueur and rum, and halve the lemon.
Ready your strawberries and place in decorative bowls. Peel the bananas, removing any
strings clinging to their flesh, only the moment
before cooking, either in the kitchen or at the
table.

The cooking

Set the chafing dish on the lighted burner
and add the butter. Let it bubble up, then
stir in the sugar and grated orange peel. Pour
in the orange juice and, with drama, pierce
the cut side of a lemon half with your fork
as you squeeze in the juice from on high,
repeating with the second lemon half. Pour
in the orange liqueur—from the bottle, if you
can judge the amount of approximately 5
tablespoons. Let the liquid bubble up, then
arrange the bananas in the pan. Baste them
with the liquid almost continuously as it
cooks and bubbles and gradually turns into a
thick syrup, almost a caramel. This will take
some 5 minutes of basting and animated
conversation. However, do not cook the
bananas too much or they will be too limp to
transfer from chafing dish to platter or plates.

The flaming finish, and serving

As soon as you conclude the bananas are
done and the syrup is thick enough, pour in
the rum or whiskey, let bubble up, then
either tip the pan into the flame, or ignite
with a lighted match. Spoon the flaming liquid
over the bananas until the flames subside. Arrange them either on a platter and decorate
with strawberries as illustrated, or serve onto
individual plates. Baste bananas and strawberries with the syrup.

Baste bananas frequently with the syrup as they cook.

⏱ *Timing*

Long before you ever thought of this party, you might—just as a matter of good kitchen routine—have stocked your freezer with home-grated cheese, hard-toasted French bread rounds, and good brown stock. Perhaps you've been fooling the family dog all along by freezing any leftover bones, though you'd want to add a couple of good fresh meaty ones before boiling up your hoard. It does take from 6 to 7 hours to make a meat stock, but you can set it to boil whenever you wish, and stop and start it at will. Homemade onion soup is never a last-minute decision, then, but since so much can be prepared beforehand, including the onions (several days), it's not a last-minute job either.

The day before you serve Cobb Salad, you can poach and chill the chicken breasts, then dice them, as well as cooking and dicing the bacon and the eggs. You can also wash, dry, and refrigerate the greens.

In the late afternoon, organize your chafing dish tray, but keep the butter, orange peel, and juice refrigerated. Peel the tomatoes, make the vinaigrette, and prepare the cheese for the onion soup.

An hour before your guests come, prepare the tureen or bowls for the onion soup, except for the topping. Finish the topping and slip the tureen into the oven 45 minutes (20 to 25 for individual bowls) before supper. Then dice your salad greens, tomatoes, and avocado.

Just before dinner, arrange the salad bowl and prepare the egg yolk and wine mixture for the tabletop finish of your gratin. Peel bananas just before you cook them.

Menu Variations

The recipe gives you three ways of serving *onion soup*, whether homemade or canned; some other hearty soups are mentioned in the Leftovers section below.

Cobb Salad, if you beef it up as suggested in the recipe, can be almost a supper in itself—a lunch, certainly. Other sturdy salads might well follow onion soup: a beef salad *à la parisienne;* a turkey salad; chicken salad; fish and shellfish salads; lentil and dried bean salads; *salade niçoise* with tuna, oil-cured black olives, egg, and anchovy. Other composed salads, like a *salade à la d'Argenson* of rice and beets, or a vegetable salad of the season, might need some additions, like fish, meat, poultry, cheese, or chick-peas. You might arrange a pretty Greek salad, with zucchini and porphyry-purple Calamata olives snowed with feta cheese. If you enjoy the speckled, sparkly look of Cobb Salad but want something lighter, try dicing colorful raw vegetables for an old-fashioned Calico Salad. An amusing variant, nice with cold ham, is blanched chopped carrots with blanched shredded red cabbage, cooled and marinated in a sweet-sour vinaigrette or sour cream dressing.

For other chafing dish *desserts*, there are always sweet omelets, and crêpes Suzette, and ice cream bathed in hot blazing fruits or flaming sauces.

Leftovers

French *onion soup* has as many cheerful consequences as saying "I do." That meat you might have removed when just tender from your possibly meaty soup bones could in itself become a small boiled dinner, or could make a fine hash. But beef stock aside, you can do a lot with leftover onion soup. You can add cooked rice or potatoes to it, with some cream, and process the whole lot for a soubise soup. If you strain out the onions, you have a delicious, freezable broth to add to other soups, or to sauces or stews (if not already oniony); and you might even clarify it and reduce it to make an aspic coating for the likes of chicken livers or duck. The beef broth, if you made extra, is of course a kitchen fundamental, as acknowledged in the French term *fonds de cuisine*. The toast rounds can be frozen or refrozen, as can the grated cheese; and the cooked cheese topping can be puréed, to be added as thickening to the same soup, or to another soup another day.

You can't keep a finished, tossed *Cobb Salad*, but you could simmer its remains in those of an onion soup for a sort of "Robert Cobb minestrone." If you diced but did not dress more ingredients than you needed after all, they can be put to excellent use. The lettuce and greens can be tossed into a *potage santé* or a vegetable broth (the French heal-all for a cold or an upset stomach). You dice a turnip, an onion, two carrots, a large potato, and very little parsley, add lettuce if you have it, and simmer in water for 20 minutes, then strain. It's pallid but pleasant, and it does stay down. Extra avocado can be run through the processor with a scallion or small onion, lemon juice, salt and red pepper to taste, and a little cream cheese, if you like, for thickening; this gives you a version of guacamole. It also stuffs cherry tomatoes, as does a mixture of minced hard-boiled egg, bacon, and chives, bound with mayonnaise. That same mixture, without the mayonnaise but with browned buttery crumbs, makes a nice garnish for cooked broccoli or spinach. Extra diced tomatoes can be simmered briefly in oil or butter and herbs for a delicious sauce.

If you have extra bananas and don't want to take them straight, you could process them with cream, lemon, rum, and sugar, then chill for a mousse or freeze for a sort of ice cream. Or use them in a fruit cup or, if they've ripened a bit, make banana bread. Finally, mine eyes have actually seen sandwiches of peanut butter and bananas—but this is more a dare than a suggestion!

Postscript: *Una furtiva lagrima*

Often before the piano, as French chefs call their stoves, I shed a furtive tear—not because I'm lovelorn like the poor tenor in *L'Elisir d'Amore,* but because I have onions to cut. So I took up the topic in my column in *McCall's* magazine, hoping my friendly correspondents would have some helpful ideas. I've learned a lot over the years from their letters. This time I got no fewer than 19 suggestions, every one guaranteed surefire. Space prevents my quoting them all, but here are a few.

Hold your breath while slicing, so that you don't breathe in the vapors. Slice by candle-light, and the vapors will be burned off by the flame. Hold a match between your teeth, flint end sticking out. Stand with a fan behind you and an open window in front of you. Keep your mouth open. Keep your mouth closed.

I've tried them all, to not much effect; but onions are worth a tear or two and, besides, one of these days I'll make my way to a sporting-goods store, to equip myself for a final experiment. One writer says she just puts on a diving mask or swimming goggles. "It looks funny," she says, "but it really works." I bet it does.

Appendix

Butter

Butter substitutes
There is no substitute for the taste of good butter in cookery. However, if you are using other spreads, they usually react in the same manner as butter, and you can use them interchangeably.

Clarified Butter:
Since butter is made from cream, a certain residue of milk particles remains in it after churning — more or less, depending on the quality of the butter. It is this milky residue that blackens when the butter is over-heated, giving the butter itself and anything that cooks with it a speckled look and a burned taste. Therefore, if you are to brown anything in butter alone, you must clarify it, meaning that you rid the butter of its milky residue. Although you can clarify it by letting it melt and spooning the clear yellow liquid off the residue, which sinks to the bottom of the pan, you are getting only a partial clarification because much of the yellow liquid remains suspended in the residue. You are far better off actually cooking the butter, which coagulates the milk solids and evaporates the water content. Here is how to go about it.

To clarify butter
For about 1½ cups (3½ dL)

1 pound (450 g) butter

Equipment:
A 2-quart (2 L) saucepan; a small sieve lined with 3 thicknesses of washed cheesecloth; a screw-topped storage jar

For even melting, cut the butter into smallish pieces and place in the saucepan over moderate heat. When butter has melted, let it boil slowly, watching that it does not foam up over rim of pan. Listen to it crackle and bubble, and in a few minutes the crackling will almost cease — at this point, too, the butter may rise up in a foam of little bubbles. The clarification has been accomplished: the water content of the milky residue has evaporated, and if you continue to boil it, the butter will start to brown. Remove from heat at once and let cool a few minutes. Then strain through lined sieve into jar. You should have a beautifully clear deep yellow liquid, which will congeal and whiten slightly as it cools.

Clarified butter will keep for months in the refrigerator in a closed container. Scoop out what you want to use, and you may want to heat and liquefy it before using. (This clarified butter is the same as the *ghee* used in Indian cookery.)

Salad Dressings

Vinaigrette:
Basic French dressing for salads, cold vegetables, and so forth
For ½ cups (1 dL), enough for 6

1 to 2 Tb excellent wine vinegar and/or lemon juice

¼ tsp salt

¼ tsp dry mustard

6 to 8 Tb best-quality olive oil or salad oil or a combination of both

Several grinds of fresh pepper

Optional: 1 tsp finely minced shallots or scallions and/or fresh or dried herbs, such as chives, tarragon, basil

Either beat the vinegar, salt, and mustard in a bowl until dissolved, then beat in the oil and seasonings. Or place all ingredients in a screw-topped jar and shake vigorously to blend. Dip a piece of lettuce into the dressing and taste; correct seasoning.

Variations for Cold Fish Salads, Eggs, and Vegetables:
Garlic and lemon dressing
Purée a clove of garlic into a bowl, using a garlic press, then mash into a fine paste with the ¼ teaspoon salt and grated peel of ½ lemon. Proceed with vinaigrette as usual.

Vinaigrette with sesame paste
Make the garlic and lemon dressing, and beat in 1 teaspoon or so of sesame paste after you have added the lemon peel.

A creamy dressing
Make the dressing as usual, but also beat in an egg white or an egg yolk, or a tablespoon or 2 heavy cream or sour cream before adding the oil.

Vinaigrette for a Crowd of 30:
For about 3½ cups (almost 1 L)

4 Tb minced shallots or scallions

2 Tb dry mustard

5 to 6 shakes of hot pepper sauce

Grinds of fresh pepper to taste

About 1 Tb salt, or to your taste

5 Tb wine vinegar; more if needed

2 Tb fresh lemon juice

3 cups (¾ L) best-quality olive oil or salad oil or a combination of both

Herbs, such as tarragon, basil, or chives

Prepare the dressing as described previously, but you may want to beat it up in an electric mixer.

Index

A NOTE ABOUT THE AUTHOR

Julia Child was born in Pasadena, California. She was graduated from Smith College and worked for the OSS during World War II in Ceylon and China. Afterward she lived in Paris, studied at the Cordon Bleu, and taught cooking with Simone Beck and Louisette Bertholle, with whom she wrote the first volume of *Mastering the Art of French Cooking* (1961).

In 1963 Boston's WGBH launched *The French Chef* television series, which made Julia Child a national celebrity, earning her the Peabody Award in 1965 and an Emmy in 1966; subsequent public television shows were *Julia Child & Company* (1978) and *Julia Child & More Company* (1980), both of which were accompanied by cookbooks, and from which the material in this volume is collated.

In 1989 she published *The Way to Cook*. More recently, companion books to three television series have been published: *Cooking with Master Chefs*, *In Julia's Kitchen with Master Chefs*, and *Baking with Julia*. A new television series in collaboration with Jacques Pépin, *Julia and Jacques Cooking at Home*, will be released in the fall of 1999, with an accompanying cookbook. She lives in Cambridge, Massachusetts, and Santa Barbara, California.

A NOTE ON THE TYPE

The text of this book was set in Sabon, a typeface designed by Jan Tschichold (1902–1974), the well-known German typographer. Based loosely on the original designs by Claude Garamond (c. 1480–1561), Sabon is unique in that it was explicitly designed for hotmetal composition on both the Monotype and Linotype machines as well as for filmsetting. Designed in 1966 in Frankfurt, Sabon was named for the famous Lyons punch cutter Jacques Sabon, who is thought to have brought some of Garamond's matrices to Frankfurt.